PERFECT
SAUCES

Valerie Ferguson

LORENZ BOOKS

Contents

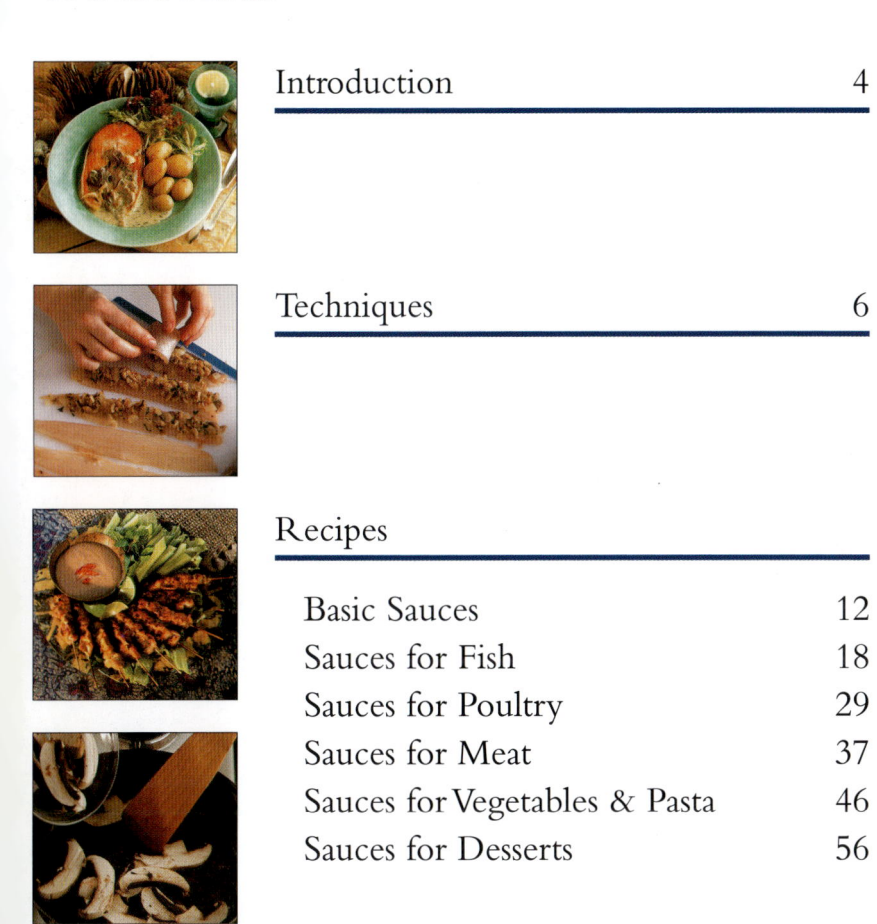

Introduction   4

Techniques   6

Recipes

    Basic Sauces   12
    Sauces for Fish   18
    Sauces for Poultry   29
    Sauces for Meat   37
    Sauces for Vegetables & Pasta   46
    Sauces for Desserts   56

Index   64

Introduction

Culinary life would be very dull without sauces. Plainly cooked food is all very well and makes a pleasant change after a spate of overindulgence, but it can become decidedly monotonous. In earlier times, before refrigerators, unadorned food was probably quite unpleasant, which is no doubt why sauces have a long history in nearly every culture renowned for its cuisine.

A sauce is generally soft and flowing, although there are exceptions; it should be rich and concentrated in flavour, well-rounded and mellow, neither too bland nor overpowering. In other words, the sauce may be thin, but the flavour shouldn't be! It should enhance the food it is served with but shouldn't overpower it. Equally, give a generous measure, but don't leave the food swimming. It's good to know exactly what it is you're eating.

Sauces can, of course, be savoury or sweet and may be an essential part of a dish or served as an accompaniment, in which case you have greater freedom. Some sauces are traditionally served with specific foods, like orange sauce with duck, and chocolate fudge sauce with profiteroles – although they could be served with other things. So if you're looking for variety with your meals, sauces cover everything!

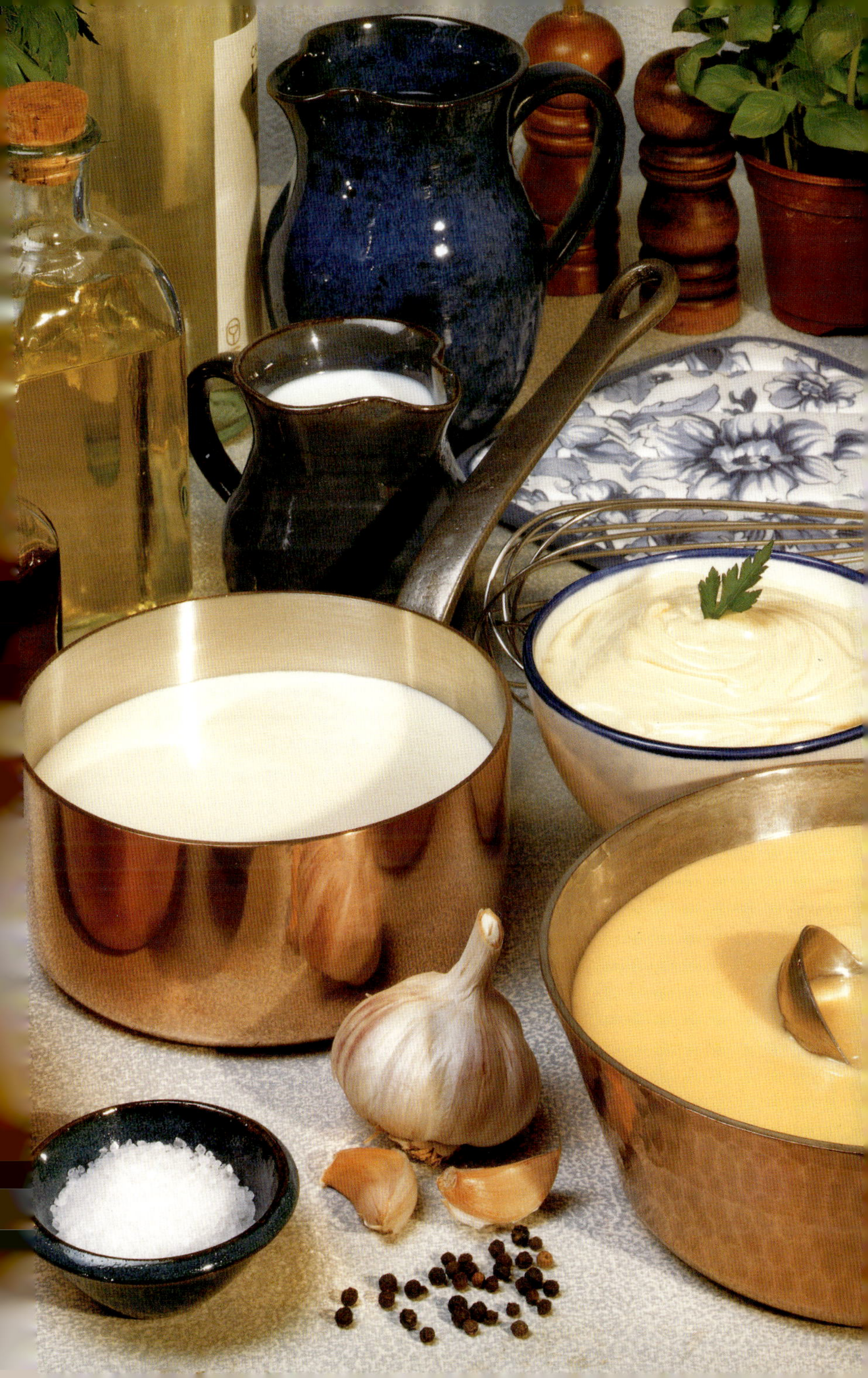

TECHNIQUES

Stocks

Many sauces depend for their depth and richness on a good-quality stock base. Fresh stock will give the most balanced flavour and it is worth the effort to make it at home. It may be frozen successfully for several months. Canned beef bouillon and chicken broth are good substitutes. For everyday cooking, most cooks will use stock cubes, but these often have a salt base, so taste carefully and season lightly.

Fish Stock

INGREDIENTS
1 carrot
1 celery stick
1 onion
any fish bones, skin and trimmings available
6 black peppercorns
2 bay leaves
3 parsley stalks

1 Scrub the carrot and celery. Using a sharp knife, coarsely slice the onion, chop the carrot and slice the celery into even-sized pieces.

2 Place all the ingredients in a large pan and add enough water to cover. Bring to the boil, skim the surface and simmer the stock, uncovered, for 20 minutes.

3 Strain and use immediately or store for 2 days in the refrigerator.

Brown Stock

INGREDIENTS
30 ml/2 tbsp vegetable oil
1.5 kg/3–3½ lb shin, shank or
 neck of beef bones,
 cut into pieces
225 g/8 oz shin of beef,
 cut into pieces
1 bouquet garni
2 onions, quartered
2 carrots, chopped
2 celery sticks, sliced
5 ml/1 tsp black peppercorns
2.5 ml/½ tsp salt

1 Preheat the oven to 220°C/425°F/ Gas 7. Drizzle the vegetable oil over the bottom of a roasting tin (pan) and add the bones and meat. Coat in the oil and bake for 25–30 minutes, or until well browned, turning regularly during cooking.

2 Transfer the meat and bones to a large pan, add the remaining ingredients and cover with 3.2 litres/ 5½ pints/14 cups water. Bring to the boil, skim the surface with a spoon, then partially cover and simmer for 2½–3 hours, or until reduced to 1.6 litres/2¾ pints/6½ cups.

3 Strain the stock into a bowl. Cool and remove the solidified fat before use. The stock can be stored for up to 4 days in the refrigerator.

TECHNIQUES

Chicken or White Stock

INGREDIENTS
1 onion
4 cloves
1 carrot
2 leeks
2 celery sticks
1 chicken carcass, cooked or raw,
   or 675 g/1½ lb veal bones,
   cut into pieces
1 bouquet garni
8 black peppercorns
2.5 ml/½ tsp salt

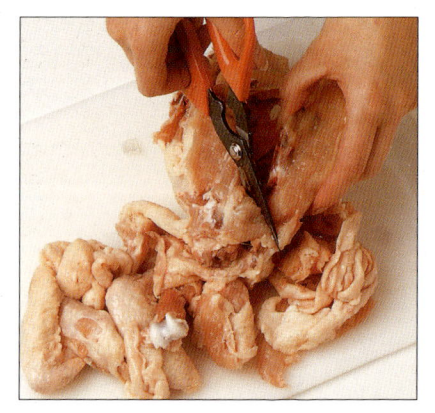

2 Break up the chicken carcass. Add the pieces, or the veal bones, if using, to the vegetables with the remaining ingredients.

1 Cut the onion into quarters and spike each quarter with a clove. Roughly chop the remaining vegetables. Place all the vegetables in a large pan.

3 Cover with 1.75 litres/3 pints/ 7½ cups water. Bring to the boil, skim the surface and simmer, partially covered, for 2 hours. Strain the stock into a bowl and allow to cool. When cold, remove the hardened fat before using. Store the stock for up to 4 days in the refrigerator.

TECHNIQUES

Vegetable Stock

INGREDIENTS
1 onion
2 carrots
2 large celery sticks, plus any small amounts from the following: leeks, celeriac, parsnip, turnip, cabbage or cauliflower trimmings, mushroom peelings
30 ml/2 tbsp vegetable oil
1 bouquet garni
6 black peppercorns

1 Halve and slice the onion. Roughly chop the remaining vegetables into approximately 5 mm/¼ in chunks.

2 Heat the oil in a large pan and fry the onion and vegetables until soft and lightly browned. Add the remaining ingredients and cover with 1.75 litres/3 pints/7½ cups water.

3 Bring to the boil, skim the surface, then partially cover and simmer for 1½ hours. Strain the stock and allow to cool. Store the strained stock in the refrigerator for 2–3 days.

TECHNIQUES

Making Gravy

Gravy made from the juices remaining in the tin after roasting meat is rich in flavour and colour. It is a traditional accompaniment to roast meat and poultry. For a thinner sauce, an alternative method to that explained here is deglazing, where liquid is added to skimmed pan juices and reduced.

1 Spoon off most of the fat from the roasting tin (pan). Set the tin over moderately high heat on top of the stove. When the juices begin to sizzle, add flour and stir to combine.

2 Cook until the mixture forms a smooth, brown paste. Add stock or other liquid used in the specific recipe and bring to the boil, stirring or whisking constantly. Simmer until the gravy has the right consistency, then season with salt and pepper.

Keeping Sauces Warm

There is nothing more unappetizing than a congealed sauce, so keeping sauces warm is essential. It can sometimes be tricky: the more delicate cream- and butter-based sauces curdle easily, and flour-based sauces may thin with prolonged heating. Follow the advice below.

1 Pour the sauce into a double boiler or a bowl suspended over a pan of simmering, but not boiling, water and leave until required. To prevent a skin forming on a cream or butter sauce, cover the surface with buttered greaseproof (waxed) paper. For flour-based sauces, spoon over a little melted butter. For sweet sauces, sprinkle the surface with caster (superfine) sugar.

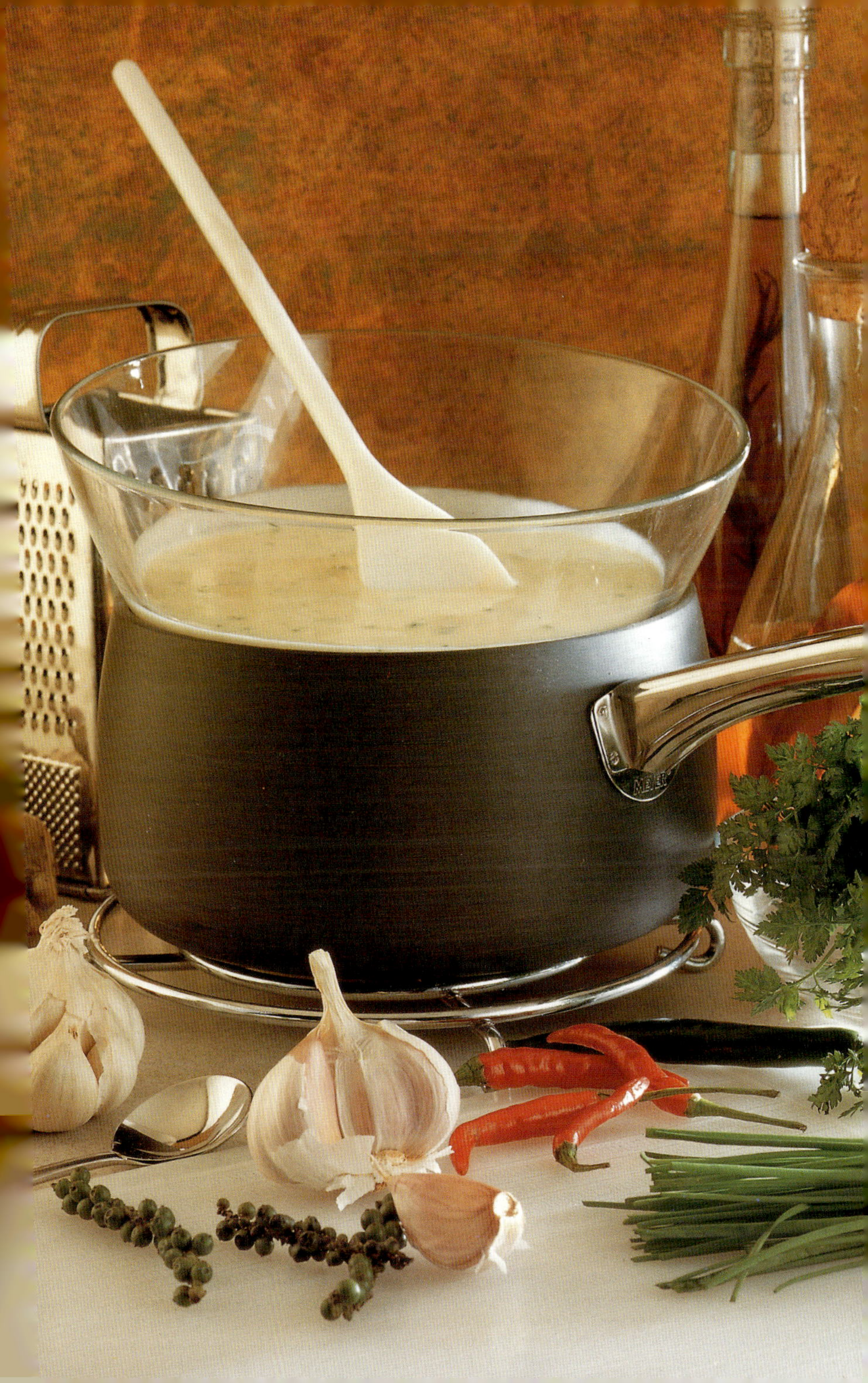

BASIC SAUCES

Mint Sauce

Tart, yet sweet, this simple sauce is the perfect foil to rich meat. It's best served, of course, with the new season's roast lamb, but is also wonderful with grilled lamb chops or pan-fried duck.

Serves 6

INGREDIENTS
1 small bunch mint
15 ml/1 tbsp sugar
30 ml/2 tbsp boiling water
45 ml/3 tbsp white wine vinegar

1 Wash and dry the mint. Strip the mint leaves from the stalks and discard the stalks.

2 Using a sharp knife chop the leaves very finely.

VARIATION: Instead of using garden mint try apple mint or lemon mint to complement the rich taste of duck.

3 Place in a bowl with the sugar and pour on the boiling water. Stir well and allow to stand for 5–10 minutes.

4 Add the vinegar and leave the sauce to stand for 1–2 hours before serving.

BASIC SAUCES

Horseradish Sauce

This light, creamy sauce has a piquant, peppery flavour that's spiced with just a hint of mustard. It is the classic accompaniment to roast beef, but is perfect, too, with herby sausages and grilled fish.

Serves 6

INGREDIENTS
2.5 cm/1 in piece fresh horseradish
15 ml/1 tbsp lemon juice
10 ml/2 tsp sugar
2.5 ml/½ tsp dry English mustard powder
150 ml/¼ pint/⅔ cup double (heavy) cream

1 Scrub the fresh horseradish and peel using a potato peeler.

2 Grate the horseradish as finely as you can.

VARIATION: Horseradish sauce is also particularly pleasing with nut-based vegetarian recipes, such as nut roasts or cutlets.

3 Mix together the horseradish, lemon juice, sugar and English mustard powder.

4 Whip the cream until it stands in soft peaks, then gently fold in the horseradish mixture. Transfer to a small bowl and serve immediately.

BASIC SAUCES

Cranberry Sauce

This is the sauce for roast turkey, but don't just keep it for festive occasions. The vibrant colour and tart taste are perfect partners to any white roast meat and it makes a great addition to a chicken sandwich.

Serves 6

INGREDIENTS
1 orange
225 g/8 oz cranberries
225 g/8 oz/1¼ cups sugar

1. Pare the rind (zest) thinly from the orange, taking care not to remove any white pith. Squeeze the juice from the orange.

2. Place the orange-rind strips and juice in a medium saucepan with the cranberries. Add the sugar and 150 ml/¼ pint/⅔ cup water to the pan.

3. Bring to the boil, stirring until the sugar has dissolved, then simmer for 10–15 minutes, or until the cranberries burst.

4. Remove the orange rind and allow to cool before serving.

VARIATION: For a stronger citrus taste substitute the pared rind (zest) of half a lemon for half the orange rind.

Bread Sauce

Smooth and surprisingly delicate, this old-fashioned sauce is traditionally served with roast chicken, turkey and game birds. For a less strong flavour, reduce the number of cloves and add a little grated nutmeg.

Serves 6

INGREDIENTS
1 small onion
4 cloves
1 bay leaf
300 ml/½ pint/1¼ cups milk
115 g/4 oz/2 cups fresh white breadcrumbs
15 ml/1 tbsp butter
15 ml/1 tbsp single (light) cream
salt and freshly ground black pepper

1 Spike the onion with the cloves. Put it into a pan with the bay leaf and pour in the milk.

2 Bring to the boil, then remove from the heat and set aside to infuse for 15–20 minutes. Remove the bay leaf and onion.

3 Return the milk to the heat and stir in the bread crumbs. Simmer until the mixture is thick and creamy. Stir in the butter and cream, season to taste and serve.

BASIC SAUCES

Apple Sauce

Really more of a condiment than a sauce, this tart purée is usually served cold or warm, rather than hot. It typically accompanies roast pork or duck, but is also good with cold meats and savoury pies.

Serves 6

INGREDIENTS
225 g/8 oz tart cooking apples
30 ml/2 tbsp water
1 thin strip lemon rind (zest)
15 ml/1 tbsp melted butter
15–30 ml/1–2 tbsp sugar

4 Stir in the butter and add sugar according to taste. Allow to cool a little before serving.

1 Using a sharp knife, peel, core and slice the cooking apples.

2 Place the cooking apples in a pan with the water and lemon rind. Cook, uncovered, over a low heat until very soft, stirring occasionally.

3 Remove the lemon rind, then beat the apples to a pulp with a spoon or press through a sieve.

Simple Tomato Sauce

Tomato sauce is extremely versatile as it can be used with pasta, fish, poultry, meat and vegetarian dishes. This sauce is best made with fresh tomatoes of any variety, but also works well with canned plum tomatoes.

Serves 4

INGREDIENTS
60 ml/4 tbsp olive oil
1 medium onion, very finely chopped
1 garlic clove, finely chopped
450 g/1 lb tomatoes, fresh or canned, chopped, with their juice
A few fresh basil leaves or parsley sprigs
salt and freshly ground black pepper

1 Heat the oil in a medium pan. Add the onion and cook over moderate heat for 5–8 minutes, or until it is translucent.

2 Stir in the garlic, fresh tomatoes and 45 ml/3 tbsp water. If using canned tomatoes, add them with their juice, instead of water, and break them up with a wooden spoon.

3 Season with salt and pepper and add the herbs. Cook gently for 20-30 minutes.

4 Pass the sauce through a food mill or purée in a food processor so that it resembles a thick sauce with a few remaining chunks of tomato. To serve, reheat gently and adjust the seasoning if necessary.

SAUCES FOR FISH

Watercress Cream Sauce

The delicate green colour of this cream sauce looks wonderful against pink-fleshed fish like salmon or salmon trout.

Serves 4

INGREDIENTS
2 bunches watercress
25 g/1 oz/2 tbsp butter
2 shallots, chopped
25 g/1 oz/¼ cup plain (all-purpose) flour
150 ml/¼ pint/⅔ cup hot fish stock
150 ml/¼ pint/⅔ cup dry white wine
5 ml/1 tsp anchovy essence (paste)
150 ml/¼ pint/⅔ cup single (light) cream
salt
pinch of cayenne pepper
lemon juice

TO SERVE
4 salmon or salmon trout fillets
melted butter

1 To make the sauce, trim the watercress of any bruised leaves and coarse stalks. Blanch the remaining leaves in boiling water for 5 minutes.

2 Drain and refresh the watercress under cold running water to retain its bright colour. In a sieve, press well with the back of a kitchen spoon to remove excess moisture, then chop finely.

3 Melt the butter and fry the shallots until soft, but not brown. Add the flour and cook for 1–2 minutes, stirring continuously.

4 Turn off the heat and gradually blend in the stock, followed by the wine. Return to the heat, bring to the boil, stirring continuously, and simmer gently for 2–3 minutes.

5 Strain into a clean pan, then add the watercress, anchovy essence and cream. Warm through over a low heat. Season with salt and cayenne pepper and sharpen with lemon juice according to taste.

SAUCES FOR FISH

6 Meanwhile, brush the fish with a little melted butter and grill for a few minutes on each side until just cooked through. Pour some sauce over each fillet and serve.

VARIATION: To make rocket (arugula) cream sauce, replace the watercress leaves with 25 g/1 oz rocket leaves.

SAUCES FOR FISH

Tarragon Mushroom Sauce

The distinctive flavour of tarragon combines perfectly with mushrooms and crème fraîche to create a superb sauce for salmon.

Serves 4

INGREDIENTS
25 g/1 oz/2 tbsp butter
1 shallot, finely chopped
175 g/6 oz assorted wild and cultivated mushrooms, trimmed and sliced
200 ml/7 fl oz/scant 1 cup chicken or vegetable stock
10 ml/2 tsp cornflour (cornstarch)
2.5 ml/½ tsp mustard
50 ml/2 fl oz/¼ cup crème fraîche
45 ml/3 tbsp chopped fresh tarragon
5 ml/1 tsp white wine vinegar
salt and cayenne pepper

TO SERVE
25 g/1 oz/2 tbsp butter
4 salmon steaks
boiled new potatoes
green salad

1 To make the sauce, heat the butter in a frying pan and gently fry the shallot to soften, without letting it colour. Add the mushrooms and cook until the juices begin to flow. Add the stock and simmer for 2–3 minutes.

2 Put the cornflour and mustard in a cup and blend with 15 ml/1 tbsp water. Stir into the mushroom mixture and bring to a simmer, stirring to thicken. Add the crème fraîche, tarragon, vinegar, salt and cayenne pepper.

3 For the fish, melt half of the butter in a large, non-stick frying pan. Season the salmon steaks and cook over a moderate heat for 8 minutes, turning once.

4 Spoon the sauce over each salmon steak and serve with new potatoes and a green salad.

COOK'S TIP: Fresh tarragon will bruise and darken quickly after chopping, so prepare the herb as and when you need it.

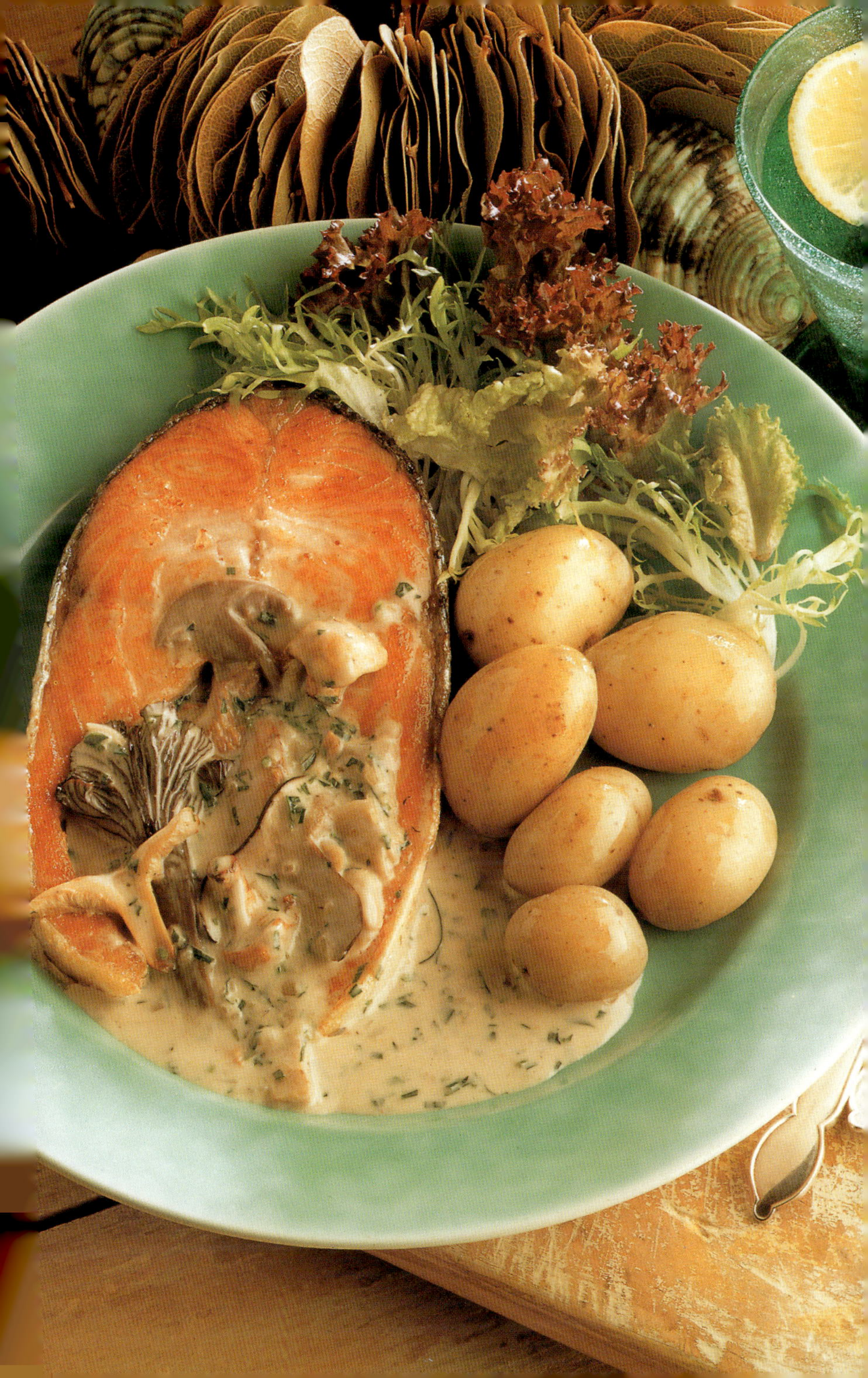

Sorrel & Vermouth Sauce

This classic, light, fluffy egg sauce, delicately flavoured with vermouth, tastes superb when served with lemon sole.

Serves 4

INGREDIENTS
50 ml/2 fl oz/¼ cup dry white vermouth
10 ml/2 tsp lemon juice
2 egg yolks
50 g/2 oz/4 tbsp butter
handful of sorrel leaves, finely chopped
salt and freshly ground black pepper

TO SERVE
50 g/2 oz/4 tbsp butter
1 small onion, chopped
115 g/4 oz/1½ cups mushrooms, chopped
50 g/2 oz/1 cup fresh brown breadcrumbs
30 ml/2 tbsp chopped fresh lemon balm
4 skinless lemon sole fillets, halved
150 ml/¼ pint/⅔ cup milk
whole sorrel leaves, to garnish

1 To make the sauce, bring a pan of water to simmering point. In a separate pan, heat the vermouth until it has reduced by half.

2 Pour the vermouth into a heatproof bowl, set it over the pan of water, add the lemon juice and egg yolks and whisk until fluffy.

3 Remove from the heat and continue to whisk while adding the butter, a piece at a time. Stir in the chopped sorrel and season to taste with salt and pepper.

4 Preheat the oven to 190°C/375°F/Gas 5. For the fish, melt the butter in a frying pan. Fry the onion and mushrooms until the onion is golden and the mushrooms have absorbed the liquid. Add the breadcrumbs and lemon balm and stir in salt and pepper to taste.

5 Place the pieces of lemon sole on a board and spread some of the mushroom mixture on each. Roll up the fish pieces carefully from head to tail and pack them tightly in a shallow casserole.

6 Pour the milk over, cover and bake for 15 minutes. Lift the fish carefully from the casserole and place on individual warmed plates. Serve with the sauce, garnished with whole sorrel leaves.

COOK'S TIP: If the sauce separates, whisk in another egg yolk.

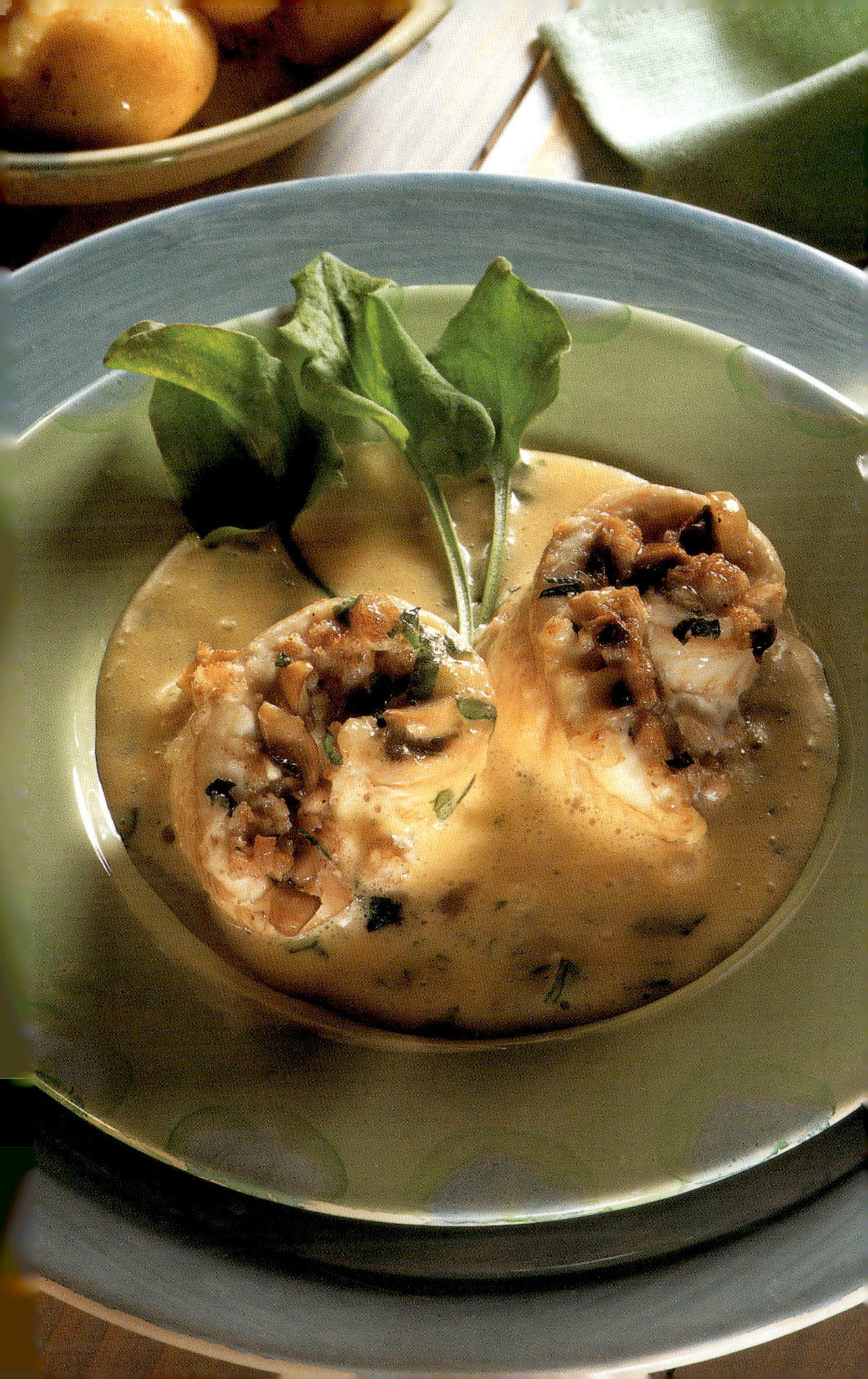

Coriander-lime Butter Sauce

More robustly flavoured fish, such as swordfish and tuna, benefit from the tastebud-tingling combination of fresh coriander (cilantro) and lime.

Serves 4

INGREDIENTS
50 g/2 oz/4 tbsp butter, preferably unsalted, at room temperature
15 ml/1 tbsp finely chopped, fresh coriander (cilantro)
juice and finely grated rind (zest) of 1 lime
salt and freshly ground black pepper

TO SERVE
675 g/1½ lb swordfish or tuna steak, 2.5 cm/1 in thick, cut into 4 pieces
60 ml/4 tbsp vegetable oil
30 ml/2 tbsp lemon juice
15 ml/1 tbsp lime juice
steamed asparagus
lime wedges and fresh coriander (cilantro), to garnish

1 To make the sauce, put the butter in a mixing bowl and beat with a wooden spoon or electric mixer until soft. Add the coriander and lime juice and rind. Season to taste.

2 Transfer the butter onto greaseproof (waxed) paper and shape it into a neat roll. Wrap and chill until firm or wrap again in foil and freeze.

VARIATION: Other fresh herbs, such as parsley or fennel can replace the coriander (cilantro), if preferred.

3 Lay the fish steaks side by side in a shallow dish. Combine the oil and juices, season and pour over the fish. Cover and refrigerate for 1–2 hours, turning the fish once or twice.

4 Preheat the grill or prepare a charcoal fire in a barbecue.

5 Drain the fish and arrange on the rack in the grill (broil) pan, or set over the hot charcoal about 13 cm/5 in from the coals. Grill (broil) for 3–4 minutes, or until just firm to the touch, but still moist in the centre, turning the steaks over once.

6 Transfer to warmed plates. Cut the coriander-lime butter into discs and place one on top of each fish steak, so that it melts to form a sauce. Serve the fish immediately, garnished with lime wedges and coriander, and accompanied by asparagus.

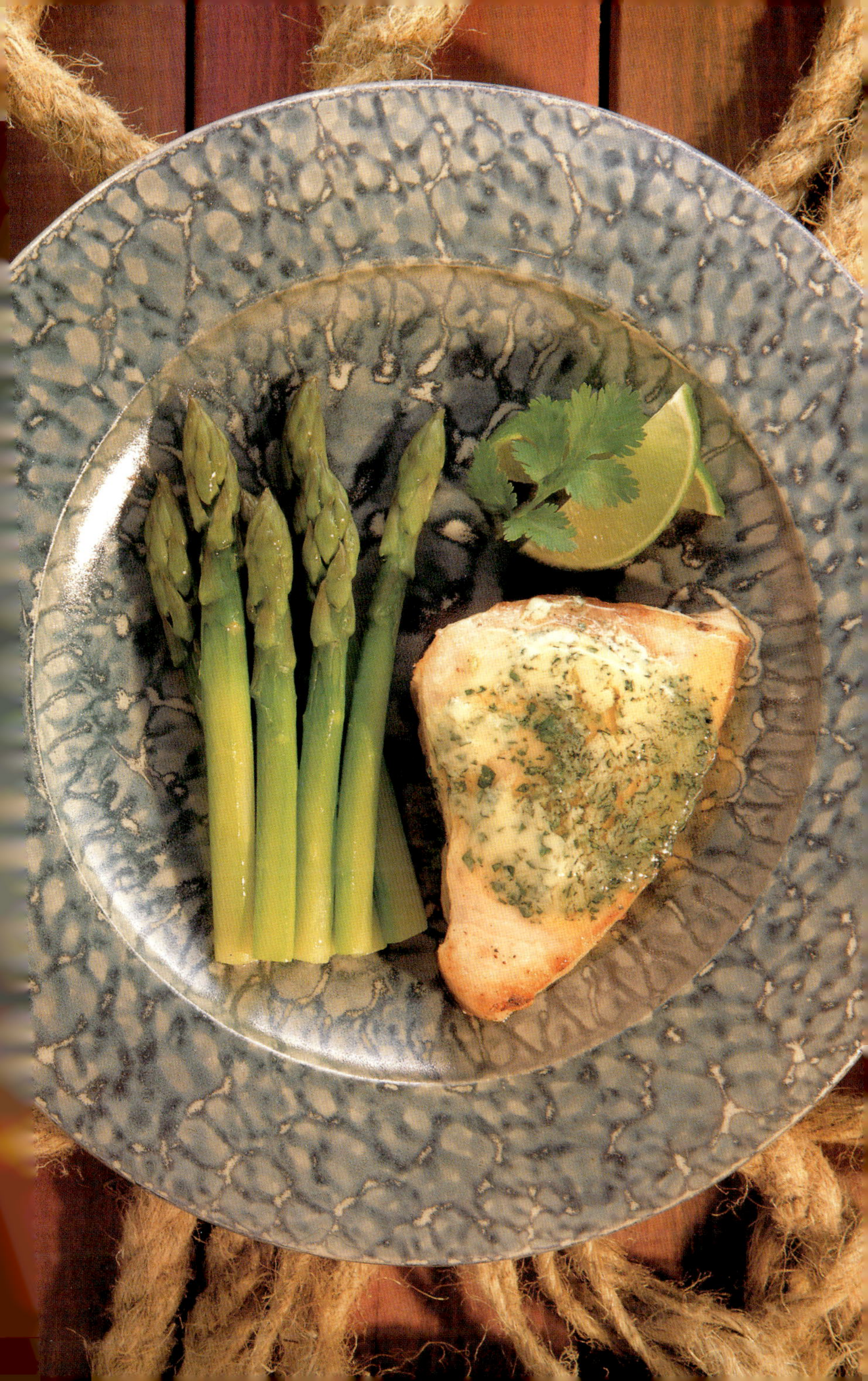

SAUCES FOR FISH

Romesco Sauce

Sweet (bell) peppers, tomatoes, garlic and almonds are the main ingredients of a Spanish sauce that is a great partner to fish and seafood.

Serves 4

INGREDIENTS
2 well-flavoured tomatoes
60 ml/4 tbsp olive oil
1 onion, chopped
4 garlic cloves, chopped
1 canned pimiento, chopped
2.5 ml/½ tsp dried chilli flakes
   or powder
75 ml/5 tbsp fish stock
30 ml/2 tbsp white wine
10 blanched almonds
15 ml/1 tbsp red wine vinegar
salt

TO SERVE
24 raw king prawns (jumbo shrimp)
30–45 ml/2–3 tbsp olive oil
lemon wedges
flat-leaf parsley,
   to garnish

1 To make the sauce, immerse the tomatoes in boiling water for about 30 seconds, then refresh them under cold water. Peel away the skins and roughly chop the flesh.

2 Heat 30 ml/2 tbsp of the oil in a pan, add the onion and 3 of the garlic cloves and cook until soft. Add the pimiento, tomatoes, chilli, fish stock and wine, then cover and simmer for 30 minutes.

3 Toast the almonds under the grill (broiler) until golden. Transfer to a blender and grind coarsely. Add the remaining 30 ml/2 tbsp oil, the vinegar and the last garlic clove and process until evenly combined. Add the tomato and pimiento sauce and process until smooth. Season with salt.

4 Remove the heads from the prawns, leaving them unshelled. Slit each one down the back and remove the dark vein. Rinse and pat dry on kitchen paper. Preheat the grill. Toss the prawns in olive oil, then grill for about 2–3 minutes on each side, until pink. Arrange on a serving platter with the lemon wedges, and the sauce in a bowl. Serve garnished with parsley.

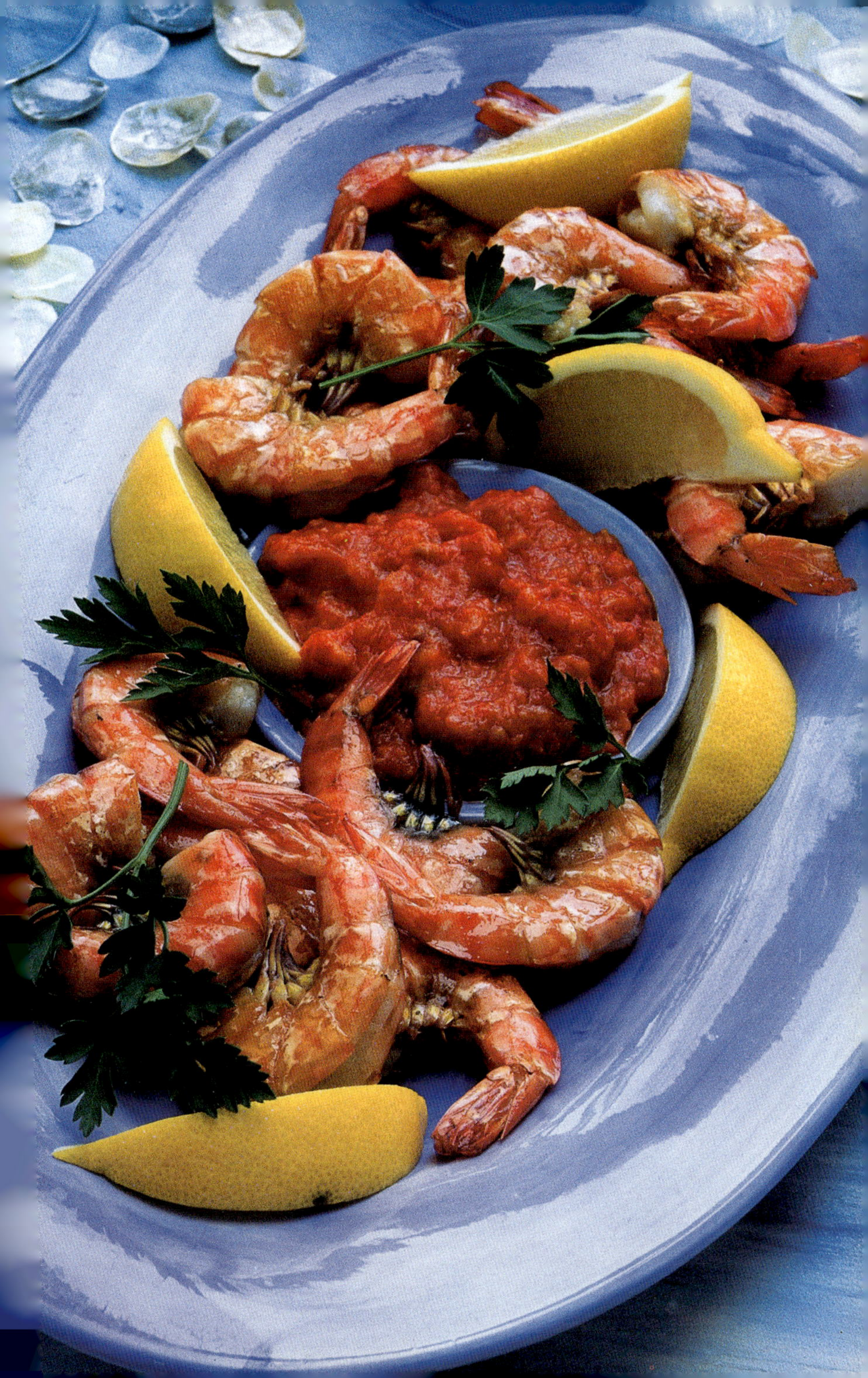

SAUCES FOR FISH

Tartare Sauce

This is an authentic sauce to serve with all kinds of fried or grilled fish.

Serves 6

INGREDIENTS
2 hard-boiled eggs, shelled
1 large egg yolk
10 ml/2 tsp lemon juice
175 ml/6 fl oz/¾ cup olive oil
5 ml/1 tsp each of chopped capers, gherkin, fresh chives, fresh parsley
salt and freshly ground black pepper

TO SERVE
grilled (broiled) or fried fish

1 Halve the hard-boiled eggs, remove the yolks and press them through a sieve into a bowl. Reserve the whites.

2 Blend in the raw egg yolk and mix until smooth. Stir in the lemon juice.

3 Add the oil very slowly, a little at a time, whisking constantly. When it begins to thicken, add the oil more quickly to form an emulsion.

4 Finely chop 1 egg white and stir into the sauce with the capers, gherkins and herbs. Season with salt and pepper to taste and serve with fish.

VARIATION: You could add the flavourings to mayonnaise.

Barbecue Sauce

Brush this sauce over chicken before cooking it on the barbecue.

Serves 4

INGREDIENTS
30 ml/2 tbsp vegetable oil
1 large onion, chopped
2 garlic cloves, crushed
400 g/14 oz can tomatoes
30 ml/2 tbsp Worcestershire sauce
15 ml/1 tbsp white wine vinegar
45 ml/3 tbsp honey
5 ml/1 tsp dry English mustard
2.5 ml/½ tsp chilli seasoning or mild chilli powder
salt and freshly ground black pepper

TO SERVE
chicken portions

1 To make the sauce, heat the oil and fry the onion and garlic until soft.

2 Stir in the remaining ingredients and simmer, uncovered, for 15–20 minutes, stirring. Cool slightly.

3 Pour into a food processor or blender and process until smooth. Press through a sieve if you prefer and adjust the seasoning.

4 Brush the sauce over the chicken portions and cook them thoroughly on a barbecue or under a grill. Turn occasionally and brush with more sauce. Serve hot or cold.

SAUCES FOR POULTRY

Lemon & Tarragon Sauce

The sharpness of lemon and mild aniseed flavour of tarragon add zest to chicken dishes.

Serves 4

INGREDIENTS
1 lemon
small bunch of fresh tarragon
1 shallot, finely chopped
90 ml/6 tbsp white wine
1 quantity Velvety Savoury Sauce
45 ml/3 tbsp double (heavy) cream
30 ml/2 tbsp brandy
salt and freshly ground black pepper

TO SERVE
grilled (broiled) chicken portions wrapped in bacon
lemon wedges and fresh tarragon, to garnish

1 To make the sauce, thinly pare the rind (zest) from the lemon, taking care not to remove any white pith which will make the sauce bitter. Squeeze the lemon juice into a medium pan and place on the hob.

2 Discard the coarse stalks from the tarragon. Chop the leaves and add all but 15 ml/1 tbsp to the pan with the lemon rind, shallot and wine. Bring to the boil.

3 Simmer until the liquid is reduced by half, then strain into a pan.

4 Add the Velvety Savoury Sauce, cream, brandy and reserved tarragon. Heat, tasting and adjusting the seasoning. Serve with grilled chicken wrapped in bacon, garnished with lemon wedges and tarragon.

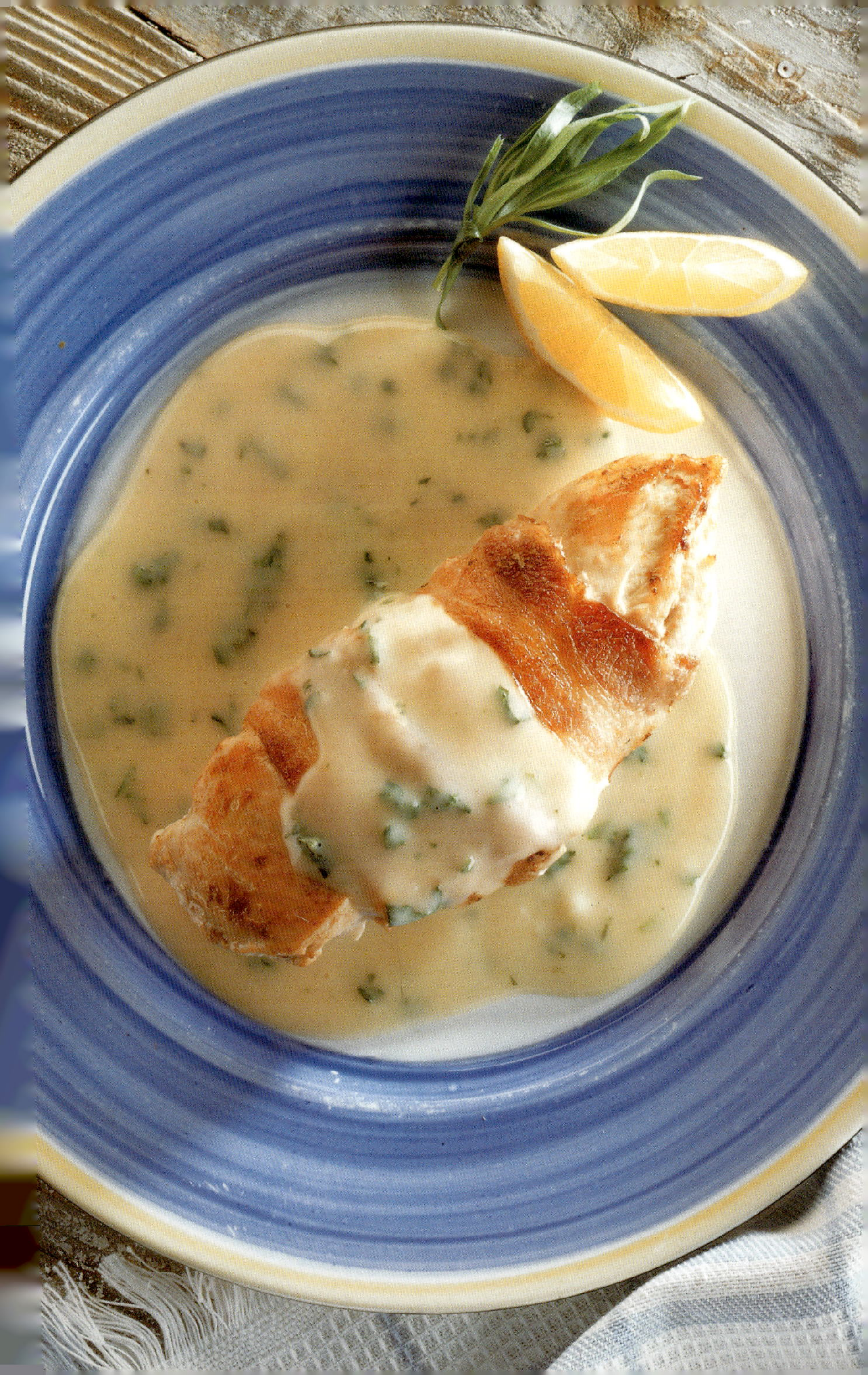

SAUCES FOR POULTRY

Peanut Saté Sauce

A traditional, spicy Thai sauce which is served with chicken.

Serves 4–6

INGREDIENTS
150 g/5 oz/scant 1 cup raw peanuts
15 ml/1 tbsp vegetable oil
2 shallots or 1 small onion, finely chopped
1 garlic clove, crushed
1–2 small chillies, seeded and finely chopped
1 cm/½ in cube shrimp paste or 15 ml/1 tbsp fish sauce
30 ml/2 tbsp tamarind sauce
120 ml/4 fl oz/½ cup coconut milk
15 ml/1 tbsp honey

TO SERVE
4 chicken breast fillets
15 ml/1 tbsp coriander seeds
10 ml/2 tsp fennel seeds
2 garlic cloves, crushed
5 cm/2 in piece lemon grass, shredded
2.5 ml/½ tsp ground turmeric
10 ml/2 tsp sugar
2.5 ml/½ tsp salt
30 ml/2 tbsp soy sauce
15 ml/1 tbsp sesame oil
juice of ½ lime
lettuce leaves
½ cucumber, quartered lengthways
1 lime, quartered
mint sprigs, to garnish

1 Cut the chicken into long, thin strips and thread, zig-zag, on to 12 bamboo skewers. Arrange on a flat plate and set aside.

2 For the marinade, dry-fry the seeds in a heavy pan. Grind smoothly using a pestle and mortar. Add the garlic, lemon grass, turmeric, sugar, salt, soy sauce, sesame oil and lime juice. Allow to cool. Spread evenly over the chicken and marinate for 8 hours.

3 To make the sauce, fry the peanuts in a wok or heavy frying pan with a little oil, or place under a moderate grill, tossing them to prevent burning. Turn the peanuts out on to a clean cloth and rub vigorously to remove the papery skins. Place the peanuts in a food processor and process for 2 minutes.

SAUCES FOR POULTRY

4 Heat the vegetable oil in a wok. Add the shallots or onion, garlic and chillies and cook until softened. Add the shrimp paste or fish sauce together with the tamarind sauce, coconut milk and honey. Simmer briefly, add to the peanuts, and process until the mixture forms a thick sauce. Transfer to a bowl.

5 When you are ready to cook, heat the grill to moderately hot. If using a barbecue, let the embers settle to a white glow. Brush the chicken with a little vegetable oil and grill (broil) for 6–8 minutes. Serve on a bed of lettuce with cucumber and lime quarters, garnished with mint and accompanied by the sauce.

SAUCES FOR POULTRY

Tangy Orange Sauce

Orange sauce is the perfect accompaniment to roast duck and rich game. For a full, mellow flavour it is best made with the roasting-tin juices, but butter makes an admirable substitute if these aren't available.

Serves 4–6

INGREDIENTS
roasting-tin juices or 25 g/1 oz/
  2 tbsp butter
40 g/1½ oz/⅓ cup plain (all-purpose) flour
300 ml/½ pint/1¼ cups hot stock
  (preferably duck)
150 ml/¼ pint/⅔ cup red wine
2 Seville oranges or 2 sweet oranges
  plus 10 ml/2 tsp lemon juice
15 ml/1 tbsp orange-flavoured liqueur
30 ml/2 tbsp redcurrant jelly
salt and freshly ground black pepper

TO SERVE
roast duck
green vegetables

1 To make the sauce, pour off any excess duck fat from the roasting tin, leaving the juices, or melt the butter in a small pan.

2 Sprinkle in the flour and cook, stirring continuously with a wooden spoon for 4 minutes, or until lightly browned.

3 Off the heat, gradually blend in the hot stock and wine. Bring to the boil, stirring continuously. Lower the heat and simmer gently for 5 minutes to allow the flavours to blend.

4 Using a citrus zester, peel the rind (zest) thinly from 1 orange. Squeeze the juice from both oranges.

5 Blanch the rind: place it in a small pan, cover with water and bring to the boil. Cook for 5 minutes, drain and add the rind to the sauce.

6 Add the juice, liqueur and jelly to the sauce, stirring until the jelly has dissolved. Season and serve with roast duck and green vegetables.

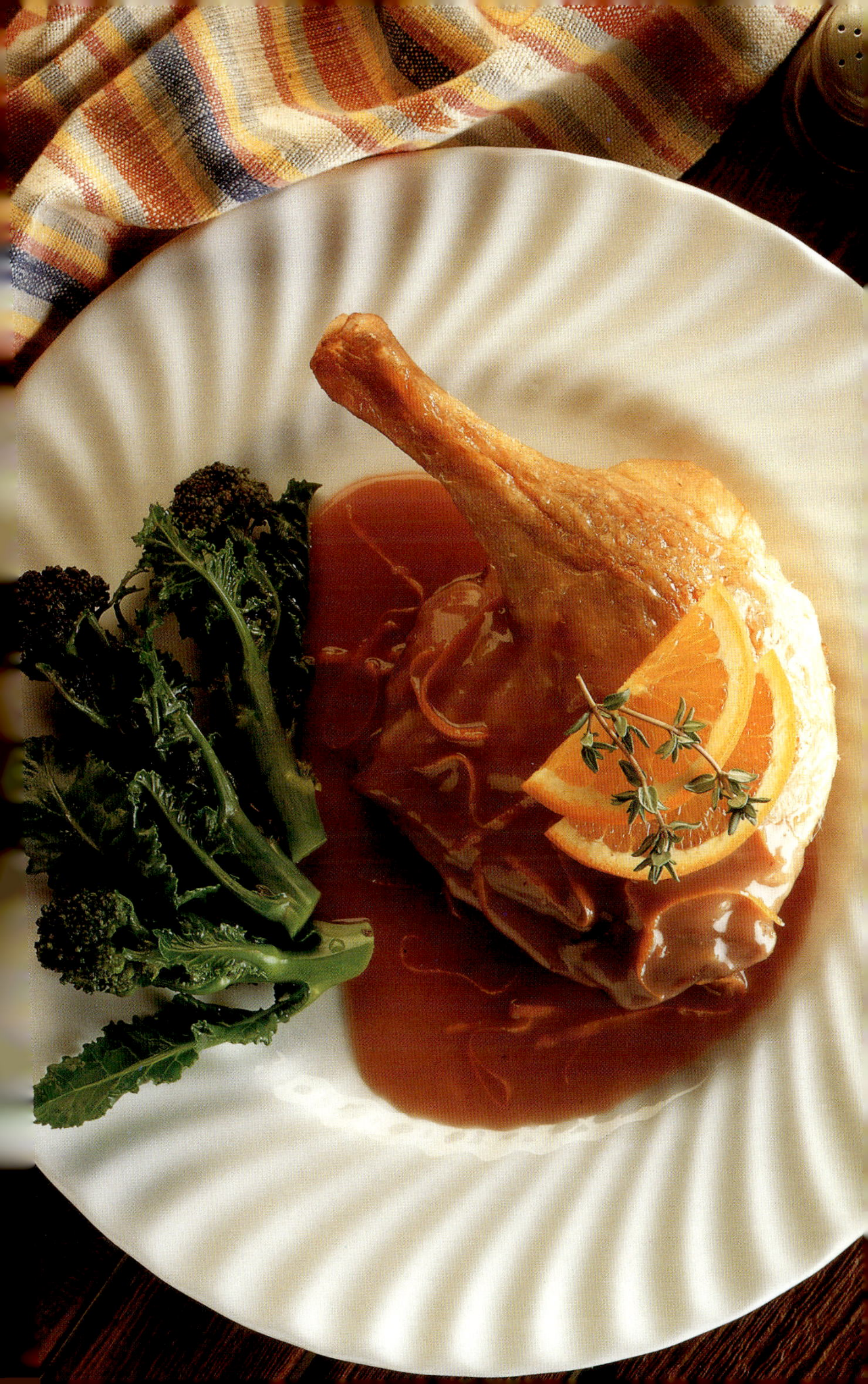

SAUCES FOR POULTRY

Velvety Savoury Sauce

A smooth, velvety sauce based on a white stock of chicken and vegetables, delicious with poultry dishes.

Serves 4

INGREDIENTS
600 ml/1 pint/2½ cups white stock
25 g/1 oz/2 tbsp butter
25 g/1 oz/¼ cup plain (all-purpose) flour
30 ml/2 tbsp single (light) cream
salt and freshly ground black pepper

TO SERVE
roast stuffed chicken and steamed asparagus

1 To make the sauce, warm the stock. In another pan, melt the butter and stir in the flour. Cook over a moderate heat for 3–4 minutes.

2 Remove the pan from the heat and gradually blend in the warm stock. Return to the heat and bring to the boil, stirring continuously until the sauce thickens.

3 Gently simmer the sauce, stirring occasionally, until reduced by about a quarter. Season to taste.

4 Skim the surface during cooking or strain through a very fine sieve.

5 Before serving, remove from the heat and stir in the cream. Serve with stuffed chicken and asparagus.

Green Peppercorn Sauce

A piquant sauce, particularly good with pork. Green peppercorns in brine are better than dry-packed ones, because they give a more rounded flavour.

Serves 3–4

INGREDIENTS
15 ml/1 tbsp green peppercorns in brine
1 small onion, finely chopped
25 g/1 oz/2 tbsp butter
300 ml/½ pint/1¼ cups light stock
juice of ½ lemon
15 ml/1 tbsp beurre manié (made by blending 7.5 ml/1½ tsp each butter and flour)
45 ml/3 tbsp double (heavy) cream
5 ml/1 tsp Dijon mustard
salt and freshly ground black pepper

TO SERVE
roast pork and cooked pasta

1 To make the sauce, dry the peppercorns on absorbent kitchen paper, then crush lightly.

2 Soften the onion in the butter, add the stock and lemon juice and simmer for 15 minutes.

3 Whisk in the beurre manié a little at a time, and continue to cook until the sauce thickens.

4 Reduce the heat and stir in the peppercorns, cream and mustard. Season to taste and serve with roast pork and cooked pasta.

Cumberland Sauce

Spicy yet sweet, this colourful redcurrant sauce is tailor-made to serve with gammon and ham.

Serves 8

INGREDIENTS
1 lemon
1 orange
2 sugar lumps
150 ml/¼ pint/⅔ cup port
4 allspice berries
4 cloves
5 ml/1 tsp mustard seeds
225 g/8 oz redcurrant jelly
10 ml/2 tsp arrowroot
30 ml/2 tbsp orange liqueur
pinch of ground ginger

TO SERVE
cold, cooked gammon, sliced
mixed salad leaves

1 To make the sauce, peel the lemon thinly so that no white pith is removed. Cut the rind (zest) into thin strips with a sharp knife or scissors. Alternatively peel the lemon with a citrus zester.

2 Blanch the rind: place in a small pan, cover with water, bring to the boil and cook for 5 minutes. Drain and set aside.

3 Wash the orange, gently pat it dry with kitchen paper, then rub it all over with the sugar lumps until they are saturated with orange oil.

4 In a small pan, bring the port, sugar lumps and whole spices to the boil. Remove from the heat and cool. Strain the port into a pan, add the jelly and stir over a low heat until dissolved.

5 Blend the arrowroot with the orange liqueur and stir into the sauce. Bring to the boil and cook for 1–2 minutes, until it has thickened.

6 Remove from the heat and add the reserved lemon rind and ground ginger to taste. Cool and serve with gammon and mixed salad leaves.

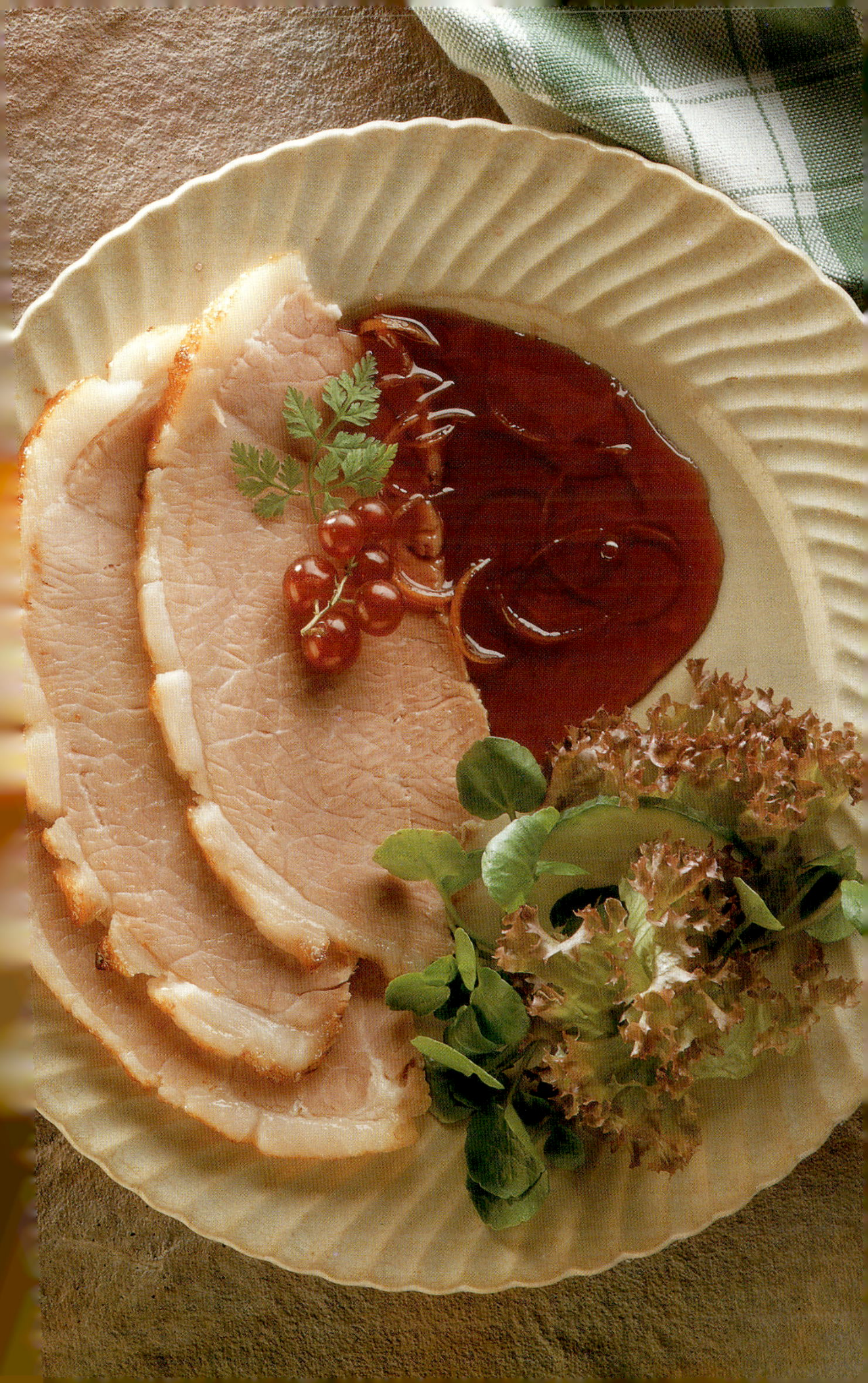

SAUCES FOR MEAT

Rich Brown Sauce

This sauce is ideal for serving with red meat, such as lamb chops, and game. It also makes a delicious, full-flavoured base for other sauces, so make a double quantity and keep some in the refrigerator.

Serves 4–6

INGREDIENTS
25 g/1 oz/2 tbsp butter
50 g/2 oz bacon pieces or streaky bacon, chopped
2 shallots, chopped
1 carrot, chopped
1 celery stick, chopped
mushroom trimmings (if available)
25 g/1 oz/¼ cup plain (all-purpose) flour
600 ml/1 pint/2½ cups hot Beef Stock
1 bouquet garni
30 ml/2 tbsp tomato purée (paste)
15 ml/1 tbsp sherry (optional)
salt and freshly ground black pepper

TO SERVE
grilled or fried lamb chops
boiled new potatoes and steamed cabbage

1 To make the sauce, melt the butter and fry the bacon for 2–3 minutes. Add the vegetables and cook for 5–6 minutes, until golden brown.

2 Stir in the flour and cook over a medium heat for 5–10 minutes, stirring continuously, until it has become a rich brown colour.

3 Remove from the heat and gradually blend in the hot stock.

4 Slowly bring to the boil, continuing to stir until the sauce thickens. Add the bouquet garni, tomato purée and seasoning. Reduce the heat and simmer gently for 1 hour, stirring occasionally.

5 Strain the sauce, pressing the vegetables against the sides of the strainer to extract the juice.

6 Skim off any fat. Stir in the sherry, if using, adjust the seasoning and serve with lamb chops, new potatoes and steamed cabbage.

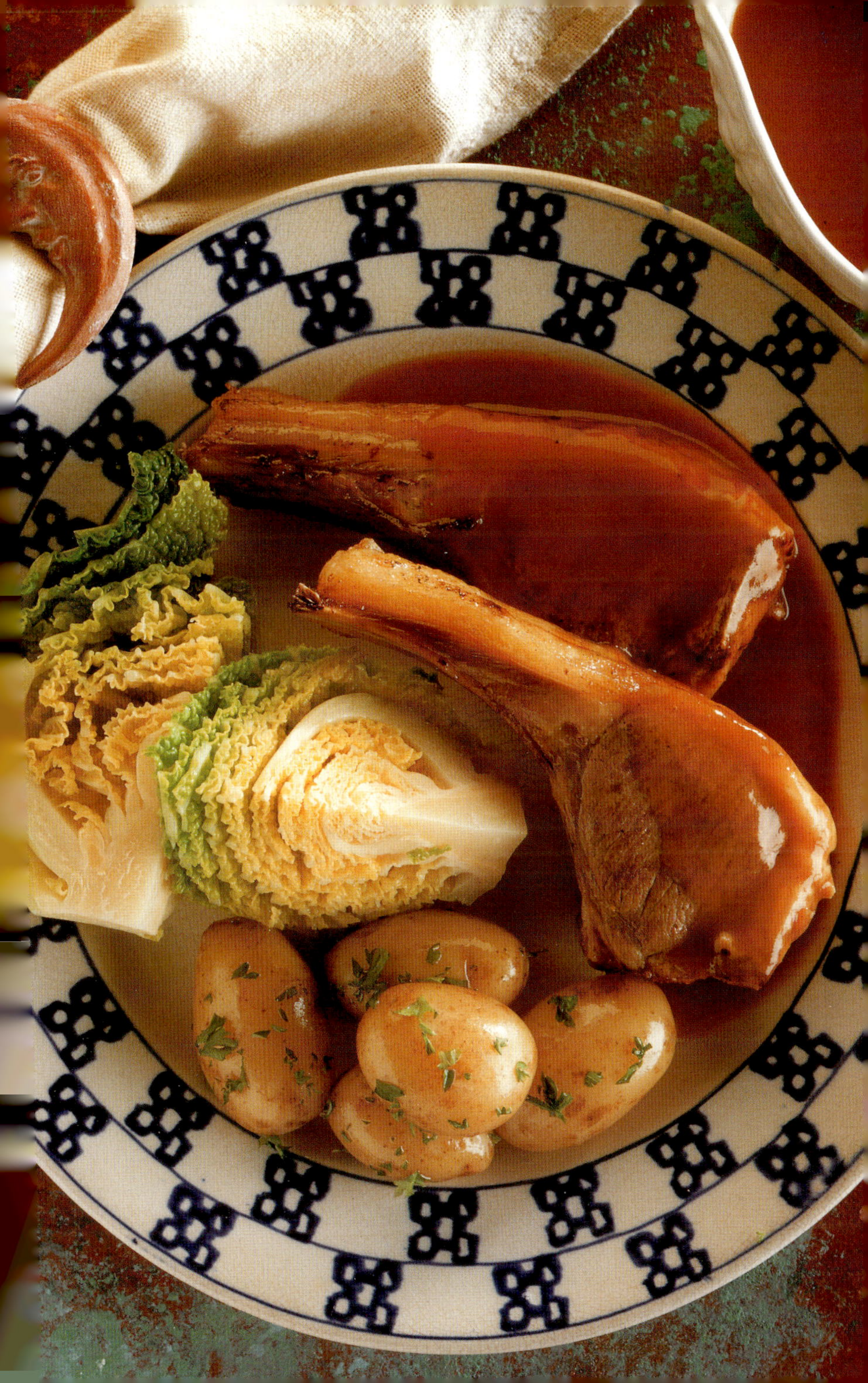

SAUCES FOR MEAT

Béarnaise Sauce

For dedicated meat-eaters, this sauce adds a note of sophistication without swamping your grilled or pan-fried steak.

Serves 2–3

INGREDIENTS
45 ml/3 tbsp white wine vinegar
30 ml/2 tbsp water
1 small onion, finely chopped
a few fresh tarragon and
 chervil sprigs
1 bay leaf
6 crushed black peppercorns
115 g/4 oz/½ cup butter
2 egg yolks
15 ml/1 tbsp chopped fresh herbs
salt and freshly ground black pepper

TO SERVE
grilled steak and mixed salad

1 To make the sauce, place the vinegar, water, onion, herbs and peppercorns in a saucepan. Simmer gently until the liquid is reduced by half. Strain and leave to cool.

2 In a separate bowl cream the butter until soft and set aside.

3 In a double pan, or a bowl, over a saucepan of gently simmering water, whisk the egg yolks and liquid until light and fluffy.

4 Gradually add the butter, half a teaspoonful at a time. Whisk until all the butter has been incorporated before adding any more.

5 Add the chopped fresh herbs and season to taste.

6 Serve warm, not hot, on the side of a grilled steak, accompanied by mixed salad.

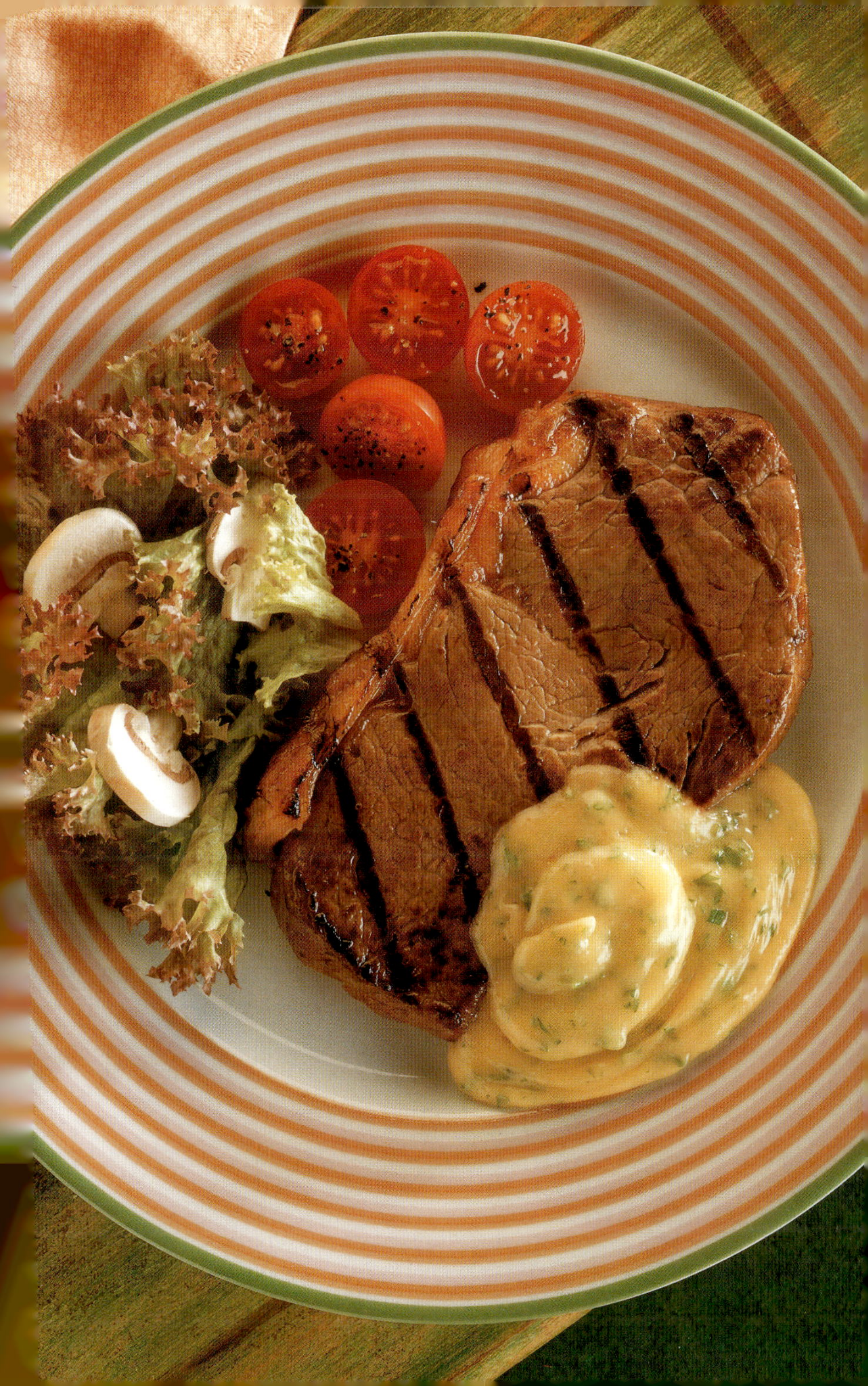

Red Wine Sauce

Black peppercorns follow the French tradition and combine well with the other bold flavours in the sauce, which is delicious served over pan-fried steak as here, or with chicken breasts.

Serves 4

INGREDIENTS
120 ml/4 fl oz/½ cup red wine
75 g/3 oz dark open-cap mushrooms, sliced
10 g/¼ oz dried morel mushrooms, soaked (optional)
300 ml/½ pint/1¼ cups beef stock
15 ml/1 tbsp cornflour (cornstarch)
5 ml/1 tsp Dijon mustard
2.5 ml/½ tsp anchovy essence (paste) (optional)
about 10 ml/2 tsp red wine vinegar
25 g/1 oz/2 tbsp butter
salt and freshly ground black pepper

TO SERVE
15 ml/1 tbsp black peppercorns
4 sirloin or rump steaks, about 225 g/8 oz each
15 ml/1 tbsp olive oil
chopped fresh parsley, to garnish
French fries
green salad

1 For the steak, crush the black peppercorns using a pestle and mortar, or coarsely grind in a pepper mill. Coat both sides of the steak with the crushed peppercorns, pressing them firmly with the palm of your hand, and brush lightly with olive oil.

2 Heat a heavy-based metal frying pan. Fry the steaks for 6–8 minutes for medium-rare or 12–16 minutes for well-done steaks, turning once throughout the cooking time. Transfer the steaks to a plate, cover and keep warm.

3 To make the sauce, pour off the excess fat from the frying pan, return to the heat and brown the sediment. Add the wine and stir with a wooden spatula to loosen the sediment.

4 Add the mushrooms to the frying pan with the dried morels, if using. Pour in the stock and cook briefly to soften.

5 Measure the cornflour, mustard and anchovy essence, if using, into a bowl. Add 30 ml/2 tbsp water and blend together. Add the cornflour mixture to the frying pan, stirring.

SAUCES FOR MEAT

6 Simmer the sauce gently until it begins to thicken, stirring all the time. Add the red wine vinegar to taste. Toss in the butter and swirl the contents in the pan with a circular motion until the butter has melted. Season to taste.

7 Return the cooked steaks to the sauce and heat through for a couple of minutes. Arrange the steaks on four individual plates, pour over the sauce and sprinkle with freshly chopped parsley. Serve with French fries and green salad.

Rich Tomato Sauce

A tasty sauce to serve with pasta or vegetables, this gives a lift to sliced courgettes (zucchini) or whole round beans.

Serves 4–6

INGREDIENTS
30 ml/2 tbsp olive oil
1 large onion, chopped
2 garlic cloves, crushed
1 carrot, finely chopped
1 celery stick, finely chopped
675 g/1½ lb tomatoes, peeled and chopped
150 ml/¼ pint/⅔ cup red wine
150 ml/¼ pint/⅔ cup vegetable stock
1 bouquet garni
about 15 ml/1 tbsp tomato purée (paste)
2.5–5 ml/½–1 tsp sugar
salt and freshly ground black pepper

TO SERVE
Sliced courgettes (zucchini)

1 To make the sauce, heat the oil and sauté the onion and garlic until soft. Add the carrot and celery and continue to cook, stirring occasionally, until golden.

2 Stir in the tomatoes, wine, stock, bouquet garni and seasoning. Bring to the boil, cover and simmer for 45 minutes, stirring occasionally.

3 Remove the bouquet garni and adjust the seasoning, adding tomato purée and sugar as necessary.

4 Use the sauce as it is or, for a smoother texture, purée in a blender. Serve with sliced courgettes.

Citrus Sauce

A delightful sauce for vegetables, such as baby courgettes (zucchini). For larger courgettes, cook whole, then halve and cut into 10 cm/4 in strips.

Serves 4

INGREDIENTS
4 spring onions, (scallions) finely sliced
2.5 cm/1 in piece fresh root ginger, grated
30 ml/2 tbsp cider vinegar
15 ml/1 tbsp light soy sauce
5 ml/1 tsp soft light brown sugar
45 ml/3 tbsp vegetable stock
finely grated rind (zest) and juice of ½ lemon and ½ orange
5 ml/1 tsp cornflour (cornstarch)

TO SERVE
350 g/12 oz baby courgettes (zucchini)

1 To make the sauce, put all the ingredients, except the cornflour, into a small pan and bring to the boil. Simmer for 3 minutes.

2 Blend the cornflour with 10 ml/2 tsp cold water and add to the sauce. Bring to the boil, stirring continuously, until the sauce has thickened.

3 Cook the courgettes in lightly salted, boiling water for 3–4 minutes, or until just tender. Drain well.

4 Pour the sauce over the courgettes and gently heat, shaking the pan to coat evenly. Transfer to a warmed dish and serve immediately.

SAUCES FOR VEGETABLES & PASTA

Pesto Sauce

Don't stint on the fresh basil – this is the most wonderful sauce in the world, unbelievably good served with pasta!

Serves 4

INGREDIENTS
2 garlic cloves
50 g/2 oz/½ cup pine nuts
50 g/2 oz/1 cup fresh basil leaves
150 ml/¼ pint/⅔ cup olive oil (not extra-virgin as it is too strong)
50 g/2 oz/4 tbsp unsalted butter, softened
60 ml/4 tbsp grated Parmesan cheese
salt and freshly ground black pepper

TO SERVE
450 g/1 lb spaghetti

1 To make the sauce, peel the garlic and blend in a food processor with a little salt and the pine nuts, until broken up. Add the basil leaves and continue mixing to a paste.

2 Gradually add the olive oil, little by little, until the mixture is creamy and thick.

3 Beat in the butter and season with pepper. Mix in the cheese. (Alternatively, you can make the pesto by hand using a pestle and mortar.)

4 Store the pesto in a screwtop jar (with a layer of olive oil on top to exclude the air) in the refrigerator until needed.

5 Cook the pasta in plenty of boiling salted water according to the packet instructions. Drain well.

6 Toss the pasta with half the pesto and serve in warmed bowls with the remaining pesto spooned on top.

COOK'S TIP: A good pesto can be made using parsley instead of basil and walnuts instead of pine nuts. To make it go further, add a spoonful or two of fromage frais.

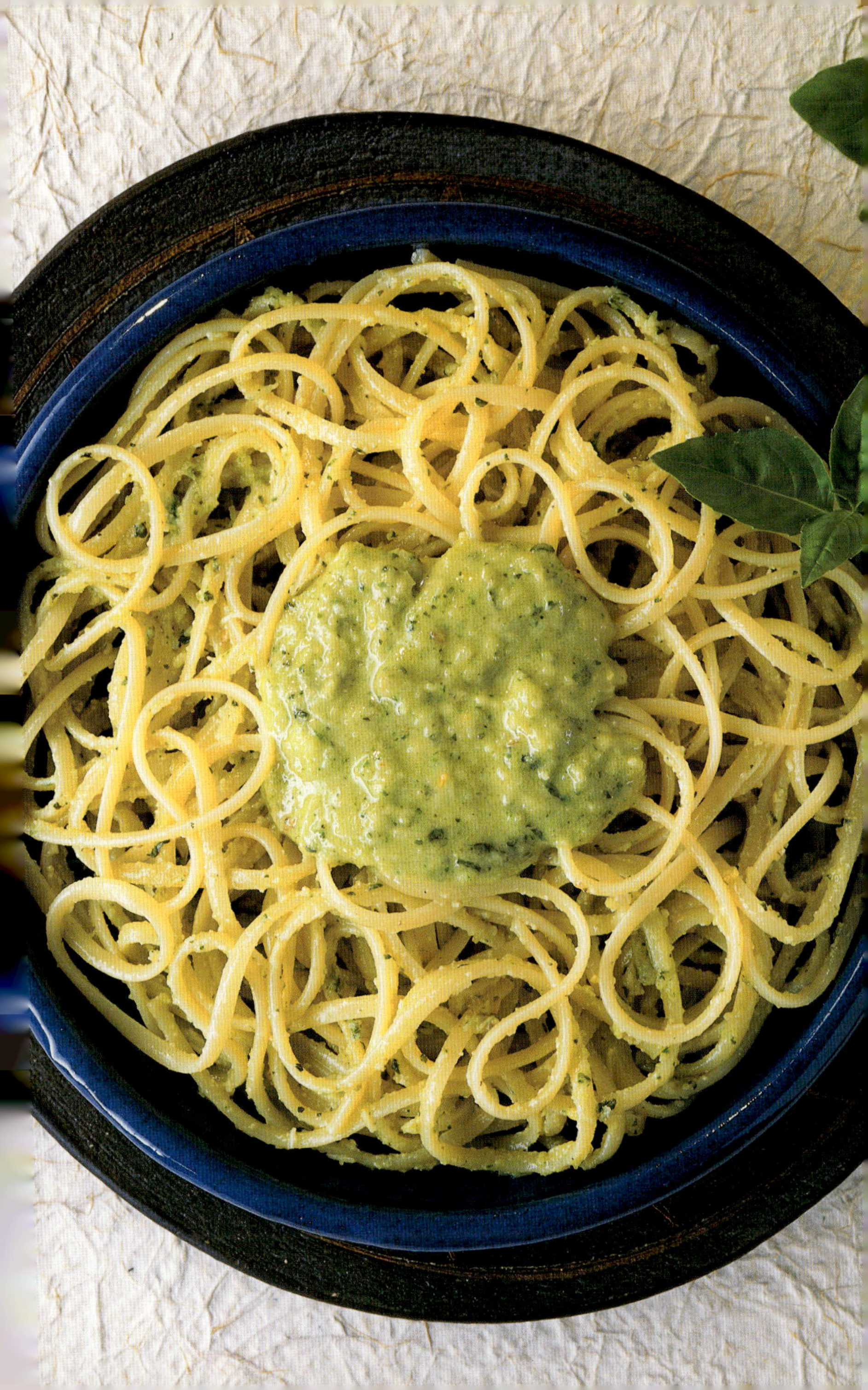

Cheese Sauce

The secret of a good cheese sauce is not to make it too thick and to stir in the cheese off the heat so that it melts gently.

Serves 4–6

INGREDIENTS
40 g/1½ oz/3 tbsp butter
40 g/1½ oz/⅓ cup plain (all-purpose) flour
600 ml/1 pint/2½ cups milk or a mixture of milk and vegetable water
150 g/5 oz/1¼ cups grated mature Cheddar cheese
grated nutmeg
salt and freshly ground black pepper

TO SERVE
1 medium cauliflower
2 broccoli heads
1 onion, sliced
3 hard-boiled eggs, shelled and quartered
6 cherry tomatoes, halved (optional)
30–45 ml/2–3 tbsp natural-coloured dried breadcrumbs

1 Divide the cauliflower and broccoli into even-size florets, slicing the thicker parts of the stalks if you prefer. Cook in lightly salted, boiling water with the onion slices for 5–7 minutes, or until just tender. Do not overcook.

2 Drain, reserving some of the vegetable water if you intend using it for the sauce. Place the vegetables in a shallow, heatproof dish and add the quartered eggs.

3 To make the sauce, melt the butter in a pan and stir in the flour. Cook for 1 minute, stirring. Gradually add the milk, or milk and vegetable water, whisking constantly until the mixture boils and thickens to a smooth sauce. Lower the heat and simmer for 2 minutes, until glossy. Remove from the heat and whisk three-quarters of the cheese into the sauce together with nutmeg, salt and freshly ground black pepper.

4 Preheat the grill (broiler). Pour the cheese sauce over the vegetables and eggs, to cover completely, and dot with the tomato halves, if using. Mix the remaining grated cheese with the dried breadcrumbs. Sprinkle the cheese and breadcrumb mixture over the vegetables and place under the hot grill, until the top is bubbling and golden brown. Serve immediately.

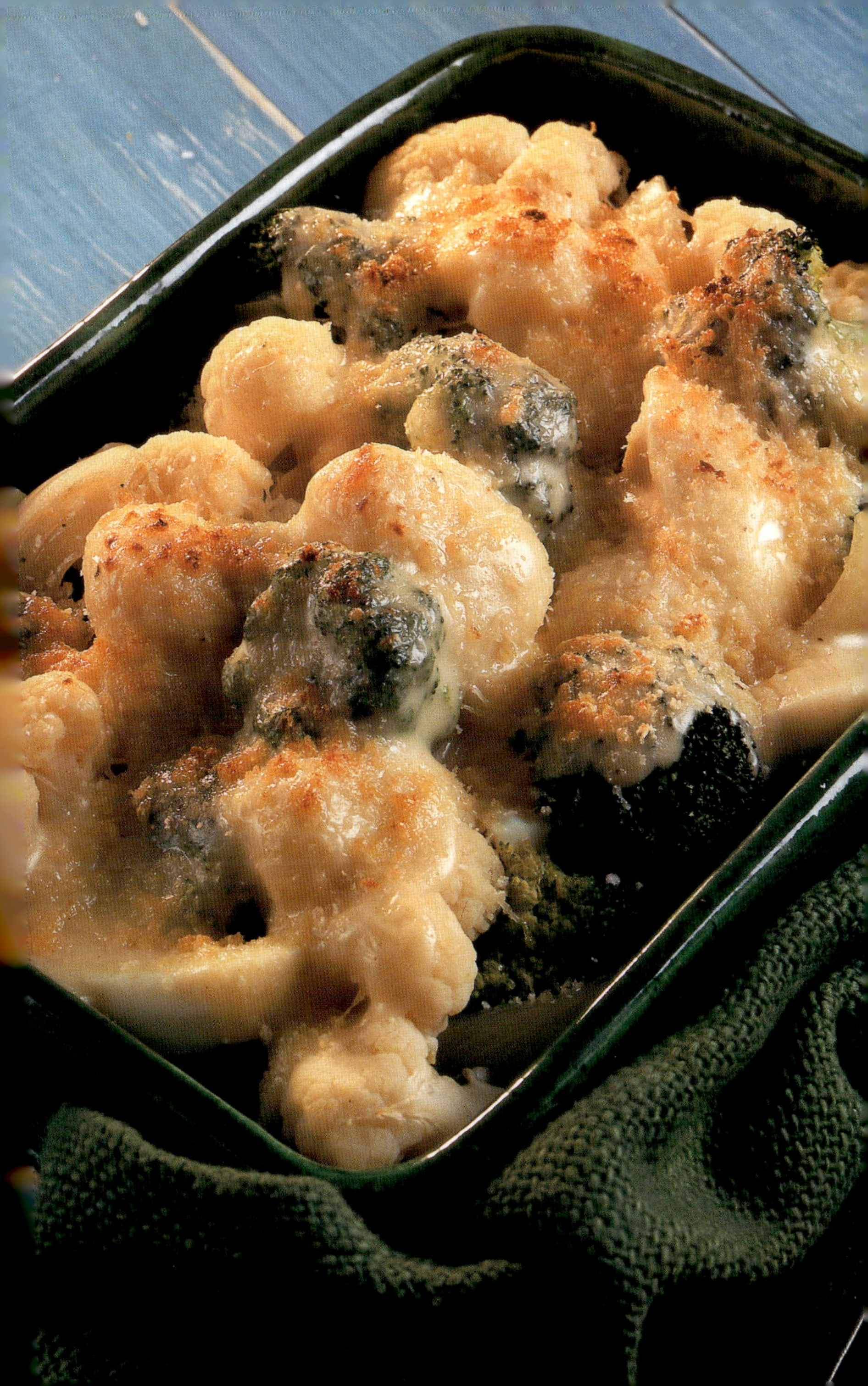

Egg & Lemon Sauce

The combination of eggs and lemon in sauces and soups is commonly found in recipes from Greece, Turkey and the Middle East. This sauce has a delicious, fresh taste and brings out the best in leeks.

Serves 4

INGREDIENTS
15 ml/1 tbsp cornflour (cornstarch)
10 ml/2 tsp sugar
2 egg yolks
juice of 1½ lemons
salt and freshly ground black pepper

TO SERVE
675 g/1½ lb baby leeks

1 Trim the leeks, slit them from top to bottom and rinse very well under cold water to remove any dirt.

2 Place the leeks in a pan, cover with water and add a little salt. Bring to the boil, cover and simmer for 4–5 minutes, until they are just tender.

3 Remove the leeks using a slotted spoon, drain and arrange in a shallow serving dish. Reserve 200 ml/7 fl oz/scant 1 cup of the cooking liquid and set aside to cool slightly.

4 To make the sauce, blend the cornflour with the cooled cooking liquid. Bring to the boil, stirring all the time, and cook over a gentle heat until the sauce thickens slightly. Stir in the sugar and then remove the pan from the heat and allow to cool slightly.

5 Beat the egg yolks thoroughly with the lemon juice and stir gradually into the cooled sauce. Cook over a very low heat, stirring all the time with a wooden spoon, until the sauce is fairly thick. Be careful not to overheat the sauce or it may curdle.

6 When the sauce has thickened, remove the pan from the heat and continue stirring for a minute. Taste, and add salt or sugar as necessary. Cool slightly.

7 Stir the cooled sauce with a wooden spoon until creamy. Pour the sauce over the cooked baby leeks and then cover and chill well for at least 2 hours. Serve sprinkled with a little freshly ground black pepper.

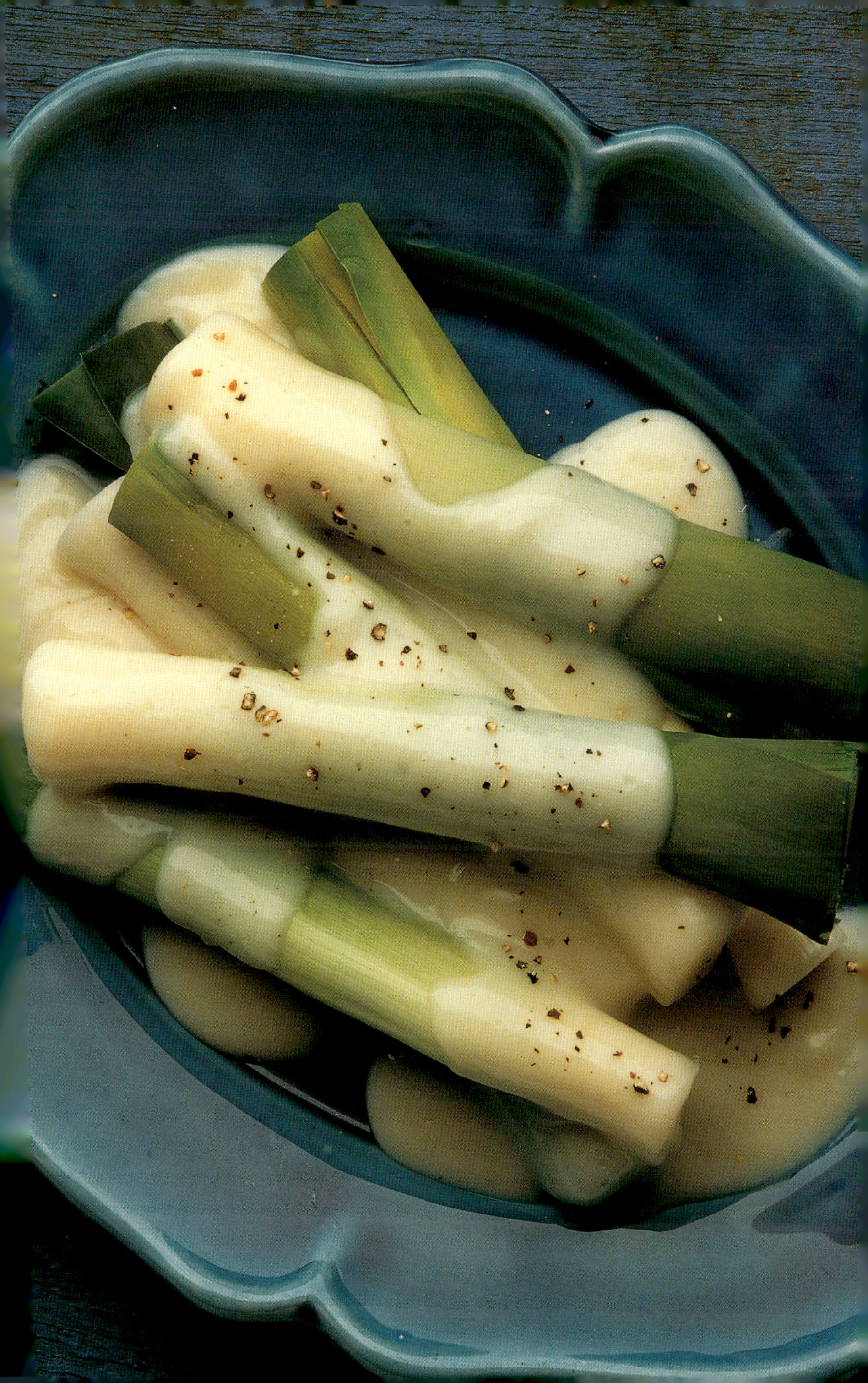

Hollandaise Sauce

A rich butter sauce which is especially good with asparagus – and fish.

Serves 2–3

INGREDIENTS
30 ml/2 tbsp white wine vinegar
15 ml/1 tbsp water
6 black peppercorns
1 bay leaf
2 egg yolks
115 g/4 oz/½ cup butter, creamed until soft
30 ml/2 tbsp single (light) cream (optional)
salt and freshly ground black pepper

TO SERVE
lightly cooked asparagus

1 To make the sauce, place the vinegar, water, peppercorns and bay leaf in a pan. Simmer gently until reduced by half. Strain and cool.

2 In a bowl sitting over a saucepan of gently simmering water, whisk together the egg yolks and reduced vinegar until the mixture is light and fluffy.

3 Gradually add the butter, a tiny piece at a time – about the size of a hazelnut will be enough. Whisk quickly until all the butter has been absorbed before adding any more.

4 Season lightly and, if the sauce is too sharp, add a little more butter. For a thinner sauce stir in 30 ml/ 2 tbsp single cream.

5 Serve the sauce immediately with lightly cooked asparagus.

Béchamel Sauce

The creamy mellowness of the béchamel makes it ideal for vegetable dishes.

Serves 4

INGREDIENTS
300 ml/½ pint/1¼ cups milk
1 small onion, finely chopped
1 small carrot, finely chopped
1 celery stick, finely chopped
1 bouquet garni
6 black peppercorns
pinch of grated nutmeg or blade of mace
25 g/1 oz/2 tbsp butter
25 g/1 oz/2 tbsp plain (all-purpose) flour
30 ml/2 tbsp single (light) cream
salt and freshly ground black pepper

TO SERVE
Steamed broccoli
Toasted almonds

1 Bring the milk, vegetables and flavourings to the boil in a pan. Set aside, covered, for 30 minutes.

2 Melt the butter in a pan. Remove from the heat and stir in the flour then cook for 1–2 minutes. Reheat the milk to almost boiling. Strain, pressing the vegetables to extract the juices.

3 Turn off the heat, and gradually blend the milk into the roux, stirring vigorously. Bring to the boil and stir until the sauce thickens. Simmer gently for 4 minutes. Remove from heat, adjust the seasoning to taste and stir in the cream. Serve poured over steamed broccoli and sprinkle toasted almonds over the top.

SAUCES FOR DESSERTS

Chocolate Fudge Sauce

A real treat if you're not counting calories. Fabulous with these profiteroles or with scoops of vanilla ice cream.

Serves 6

INGREDIENTS
150 ml/¼ pint/⅔ cup double (heavy) cream
50 g/2 oz/4 tbsp butter
50 g/2 oz/¼ cup vanilla sugar
175 g/6 oz plain chocolate
30 ml/2 tbsp brandy

TO SERVE
100 g/3½ oz/¾ cup plain (all-purpose) flour
1.5 ml/¼ tsp salt
pinch of grated nutmeg
175 ml/6 fl oz/¾ cup water
75 g/3 oz/6 tbsp unsalted butter, cut into 6 pieces
3 eggs
750 ml/1¼ pints/3 cups vanilla ice cream

1 To make the sauce, heat the cream with the butter and sugar in the top of a double boiler or in a bowl over a pan of hot water. Stir until smooth, then cool.

2 Break the chocolate into the cream. Stir until it is melted and thoroughly combined. Stir in the brandy a little at a time, then cool to room temperature.

3 Preheat the oven to 200°C/400°F/Gas 6. To make the profiteroles, sift together the flour, salt and nutmeg. In a medium pan, bring the water and butter to the boil.

4 Remove from the heat and add the dry ingredients all at once. Beat with a wooden spoon for about 1 minute, until the mixture starts to pull away from the sides of the pan, then set the pan over a low heat and cook for about 2 minutes, beating constantly. Remove from the heat.

5 Beat the three eggs lightly. Gradually add the beaten eggs to the flour mixture a teaspoonful at a time, until the dough is smooth and shiny: it should pull away and fall slowly when dropped from a spoon. You may not need to use all the eggs.

6 Using a tablespoon, drop the dough on to a buttered baking sheet in 12 mounds. Bake for 25–30 minutes, until well risen and browned. Turn off the oven and leave the puffs to cool with the oven door open.

56

SAUCES FOR DESSERTS

7 Split the profiteroles in half and put a small scoop of ice cream in each. Arrange on a serving platter or divide among individual plates. Pour the sauce over the top and serve at once.

VARIATION: Whipped cream or ready-made confectioner's custard can be used to fill the profiteroles instead of ice cream.

SAUCES FOR DESSERTS

Port Sauce

The strong flavour of this ruby-coloured sauce balances the sweetness of pears perfectly.

Serves 6

INGREDIENTS
750 ml/1¼ pints/3 cups ruby port
105 ml/7 tbsp caster (superfine) sugar
2 cinnamon sticks

TO SERVE
6 eating pears

1 Peel the pears, leaving the stalks intact. Push the end of a swivel-blade vegetable peeler into the base of each pear to a depth of about 4 cm/1½ in. Twist and remove the core.

2 Slice 5 mm/¼ in off the bottom of each pear so that it will stand upright. Stand the pears in a saucepan that will hold them comfortably but snugly. To make the sauce, add the port, sugar and cinnamon sticks.

3 Bring the port to the boil, cover, lower the heat and simmer for about 15–20 minutes, until the pears are tender. Transfer the pears to a dish and keep hot. Boil the port syrup until reduced by half.

4 Stand the pears in individual bowls, pour a little of the port sauce over and serve while still hot.

COOK'S TIP: Stacks of cinnamon sticks make an attractive decoration for this dish. Simply tie them together with gold ribbon. Long cinnamon sticks look best – they can be found in delicatessens and oriental stores.

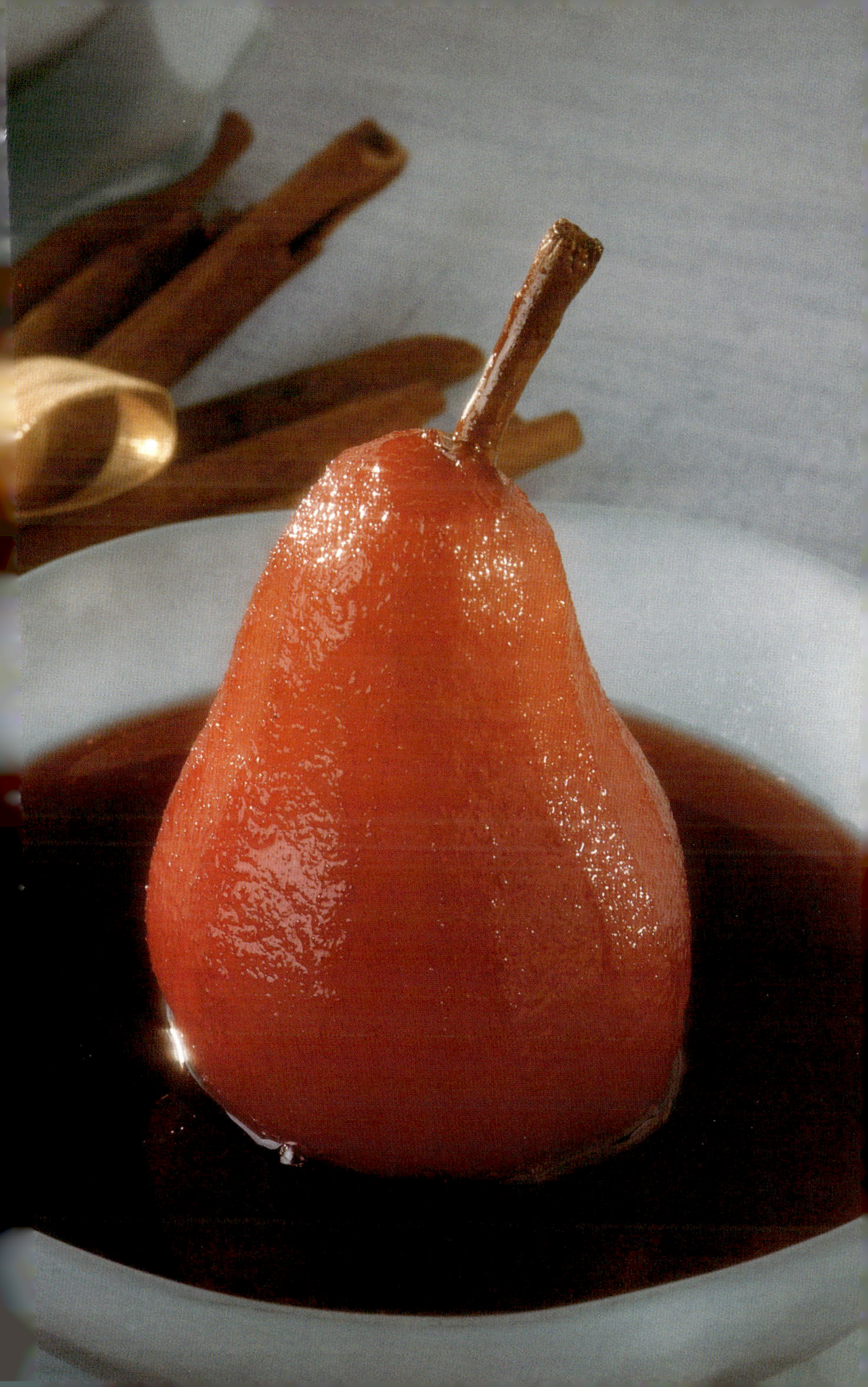

SAUCES FOR DESSERTS

Raspberry Sauce

Raspberries give a fresh, tangy taste to this sauce, which is a perfect partner to the fruit in a classic peach melba and also works well with ice cream, tarts or waffles.

Serves 6

INGREDIENTS
450 g/1 lb raspberries
15 ml/1 tbsp lemon juice
40 g/1½ oz/3 tbsp caster (superfine) sugar
30–45 ml/2–3 tbsp raspberry liqueur (optional)

TO SERVE
1 litre/1¾ pints/4 cups water
50 g/2 oz/¼ cup caster (superfine) sugar
1 vanilla pod, split lengthways
3 large peaches
vanilla ice cream, to serve
mint leaves and fresh raspberries, to decorate (optional)

1 To make the sauce, put the raspberries, lemon juice and caster sugar in a food processor fitted with a metal blade. Process for 1 minute, scraping down the sides once. Press through a fine sieve into a small bowl, then stir in the raspberry liqueur, if using, and chill.

2 In a saucepan large enough to hold the peach halves in a single layer, combine the water, sugar and vanilla pod. Bring to the boil over a medium heat, stirring occasionally to dissolve the water.

3 Cut the peaches in half and twist the halves to separate them. Remove the stones with a teaspoon.

4 Add the peach halves to the poaching syrup, cut sides down, adding more water if needed to cover the fruit. Press a piece of greaseproof paper against the surface, reduce the heat to medium-low, then cover and simmer for 12–15 minutes, until tender. Leave to cool.

5 Remove the peaches from the syrup and peel off the skins. Place on several thicknesses of kitchen paper to drain (reserve the syrup for a fruit salad), then cover and chill.

SAUCES FOR DESSERTS

6 To serve, place a peach half, cut side up on a dessert plate, fill with a scoop of vanilla ice cream and spoon the raspberry sauce over the ice cream. Decorate with mint leaves and a few fresh raspberries, if using.

COOK'S TIP: The peaches and sauce can be prepared up to 1 day in advance. Leave the peaches in the syrup and cover them and the sauce before chilling.

Sauces for Desserts

Rum-custard Sauce

Freshly ground black pepper may seem an unusual ingredient to put with a sweet sauce, until you realize that peppercorns are the fruit of a tropical vine. If the idea does not appeal, make the sauce without pepper. It is delicious with any tropical fruit, such as pineapple or mango.

Serves 4

INGREDIENTS
1 egg
2 egg yolks
30 ml/2 tbsp caster (superfine) sugar
30 ml/2 tbsp dark rum
2.5 ml/½ tsp freshly ground
   black pepper

TO SERVE
1 ripe pineapple
25 g/1 oz/2 tbsp butter
fresh strawberries, sliced

1 To make the sauce, place all the ingredients in a bowl. Set over a pan of simmering water and whisk with a hand-held mixer for about 3–4 minutes, or until foamy and cooked through.

2 To prepare the pineapple, remove the top and bottom of the fruit with a serrated knife. Pare away the outer skin from top to bottom, remove the core and cut into slices.

3 Preheat a moderate grill (broiler). Dot the pineapple slices with butter and grill (broil) for 5 minutes.

4 Arrange the pineapple slices on serving plates, scatter the strawberries over the top and serve with the sauce.

COOK'S TIP: The sweetest pineapples are picked and exported when ripe. Contrary to popular belief, pineapples do not ripen well after picking. Choose fruit that smells sweet and yields to firm pressure from your thumbs.

Index

Apple Sauce, 16
Barbecue Sauce, 29
Basil: Pesto Sauce, 48-9
Béarnaise Sauce, 42-3
Béchamel Sauce, 55
Bread Sauce, 15
Brown Sauce, Rich, 40-1
Brown Stock, 7
Butter Sauce, Coriander-lime, 24-5

Capers: Tartare Sauce, 28
Cheese Sauce, 50-1
Chicken Stock, 8
Chocolate Fudge Sauce, 56-7
Citrus Sauce, 47
Coriander-lime Butter Sauce, 24-5
Cranberry Sauce, 14
Cumberland Sauce, 38-9
Custard Sauce, Rum, 62-3

Eggs: Egg & Lemon Sauce, 52-3
Tartare Sauce, 28

Fish Stock, 6
Fudge Sauce, Chocolate 56-7

Gravy, 10

Hollandaise Sauce, 54
Horseradish Sauce, 13

Lemon: Citrus Sauce, 47
Egg & Lemon Sauce, 52-3
Lemon & Tarragon Sauce, 30-1
Lime: Coriander-lime Butter Sauce, 24-5

Mint Sauce, 12
Mushrooms: Red Wine Sauce, 44-5
Tarragon Mushroom Sauce, 20-1

Orange: Citrus Sauce, 47
Tangy Orange Sauce, 34-5

Peanut Saté Sauce, 32-3
Peppercorns: Green Peppercorn Sauce, 37
Pesto Sauce, 48-9
Port Sauce, 58-9

Raspberry Sauce, 60-1
Redcurrant jelly: Cumberland Sauce, 38-9
Romesco Sauce, 26-7
Rum-custard Sauce, 62-3

Sorrel & Vermouth Sauce, 22-3
Stocks, 6-9

Tarragon: Lemon & Tarragon Sauce, 30-1
Tarragon Mushroom Sauce, 20-1

Tartare Sauce, 28
Tomatoes: Barbecue Sauce, 29
Rich Tomato Sauce, 46
Romesco Sauce, 26-7
Simple Tomato Sauce, 17

Vegetable Stock, 9
Velvety Savoury Sauce, 36

Watercress Cream Sauce, 18-19
White Stock, 8
Wine: Red Wine Sauce, 44-5

This edition is published by Lorenz Books, an imprint of Anness Publishing Ltd, Blaby Road, Wigston, Leicestershire LE18 4SE; info@anness.com

www.lorenzbooks.com; www.annesspublishing.com

If you like the images in this book and would like to investigate using them for publishing, promotions or advertising, please visit our website www.practicalpictures.com for more information.

© Anness Publishing Limited 2013

All rights reserved. No part of this publication may be reproduced, stored in a retrieval system, or transmitted in any way or by any means, electronic, mechanical, photocopying, recording or otherwise, without the prior written permission of the copyright holder.

A CIP catalogue record for this book is available from the British Library

Publisher: Joanna Lorenz
Editor: Valerie Ferguson & Helen Sudell
Series Designer: Bobbie Colgate Stone
Designer: Andrew Heath
Production Controller: Helen Wang

Recipes contributed by: Catherine Atkinson, Janet Brinkworth, Maxine Clarke, Carole Clements, Roz Denny, Nicola Diggins, Joanna Farrow, Deh-ta Hsiung, Christine Ingram, Norma MacMillan, Norma Miller, Steven Wheeler, Elizabeth Wolf-Cohen

Photography: Karl Adamson, Edward Allwright, James Duncan, Michelle Garrett, John Heseltine, Amanda Heywood, David Jordan, Patrick McLeavey

COOK'S NOTES

Bracketed terms are intended for American readers.

For all recipes, quantities are given in both metric and imperial measures and, where appropriate, in standard cups and spoons. Follow one set of measures, but not a mixture, because they are not interchangeable.

Standard spoon and cup measures are level. 1 tsp = 5ml, 1 tbsp = 15ml, 1 cup = 250ml/8fl oz. Australian standard tablespoons are 20ml. Australian readers should use 3 tsp in place of 1 tbsp for measuring small quantities.

American pints are 16fl oz/2 cups. American readers should use 20fl oz/2.5 cups in place of 1 pint when measuring liquids.

Electric oven temperatures in this book are for conventional ovens. When using a fan oven, the temperature will probably need to be reduced by about 10–20°C/20–40°F. Since ovens vary, you should check with your manufacturer's instruction book for guidance.

Medium (US large) eggs are used unless otherwise stated.

PUBLISHER'S NOTE:

Although the advice and information in this book are believed to be accurate and true at the time of going to press, neither the authors nor the publisher can accept any legal responsibility or liability for any errors or omissions that may have been made nor for any inaccuracies nor for any loss, harm or injury that comes about from following instructions or advice in this book.